WINDJAMMER COOKING

WINDJAMMER COOKING

Great Recipes from Maine's Windjammer Fleet

Jean Kerr & Spencer Smith

Seapoint Books
An imprint of Smith/Kerr Associates LLC
Kittery Point, Maine
www.SmithKerr.com

Distributed to the trade by National Book Network.
Generous quantity discounts are available from
Smith/Kerr Associates LLC (207) 439-2921 or
www.Smith/Kerr.com

ISBN 13: 978-0-9786899-2-6
ISBN 10: 0-9786899-2-5

Text and cover design by Claire MacMaster,
    Barefoot Art Graphic Design

Printed in China

Contents

Acknowledgments

The authors would like to thank Meg Maiden, the captains, cooks, crew, and staff of the windjammers of the Maine Windjammer Association; Bud Fisher; Andy Edgar, Claire MacMaster; Kara Steere, Kathleen Rochleau, and Paula Sullivan for their invaluable help with this book. Special thanks to Frederick LeBlanc for his photographs. Visit www.FrederickLeBlanc.com.

Dedication

To all the guests, captains, and crew of the windjammers of the Maine Windjammer Association who have enjoyed and helped protect the coast of Maine.

The Windjammer Experience

SAILING A WINDJAMMER on the coast of Maine is like taking a step back in time. Back to a time before cell phones and e-mail and schedules driven by the ticking of a clock. Aboard a windjammer, the day's course is set by the direction of the wind, the tides, the currents—and by whim. Where do we want to go today? Isle au Haut on the edge of the rolling ocean? Or Somes Sound, the only fjord on the East Coast of the United States? Would this be a good day for a lobster bake on the beach of a solitary island? Or a stroll around Bucks Harbor? There's a new choice every day, and each of them is good.

Windjammers don't travel fast, but slowing down can be a good thing. On a windjammer, you have time to look at the passing scenery, to watch a school of porpoises, or to see seals sunning themselves on a rock. Windjammers give us time to read a book or learn navigation. And they give us plenty of time for great meals!

The summer winds are moderate, and have the agreeable schedule of calm in the morning, breezy in the afternoon, and calm again at night. Usually the winds are from the southwest—off the ocean—although every week or so, a northwester comes through bringing crystal clear days and crisp nights. Summer storms of any sort are rare along the coast of Maine. Even the thunderstorms that occasionally appear over land tend to dissipate when they reach the colder water.

The coast of Maine, of course, is famous for fog. That lonely point Petit Manan, only about sixty miles east of Penobscot Bay, has the dubious distinction of being the foggiest place in the United States. Fog does have its charms, however. It brings a sense of peace, isolation, and intimacy. Before modern electronic navigational devices such as radar and global positioning systems (GPS), if there was a real thick o' fog, boats tended to stay in harbor. Now, while it's sometimes pleasant to spend a relaxing day sitting in the fog, it's no longer necessary.

A Day Aboard a Windjammer

There is no "typical day" aboard a windjammer. The weather, the constantly changing scenery, raising the anchor, setting sail, and, at the end of the day, dropping anchor in a new harbor; every day is a unique experience.

For some, the day begins early. The cook is usually up before 5:00 a.m. getting the stove warmed up, prepping breakfast, and perking coffee for the early risers. Breakfast is hearty and often eaten on deck: eggs, cereal, bacon, juice, pancakes, fruit, tea, and (more) coffee are all likely to be on the menu. After breakfast, it's time to hoist the sails and raise the anchor—often a group activity. The captain may have a destination in mind for the day, or maybe the wind will determine the next harbor. Windjammers are, after all, sailing vessels, and sailing and rigorous schedules don't mix. The idea is to relax and enjoy the trip.

Passengers are welcome to help with the sailing of the ship, or they are free to take it easy—watch the islands as they slide by, or spot seals, ospreys, and maybe even a whale. Lunch is usually served on deck with both hot and cold food—the hearty breakfast being long forgotten. Afternoon is the prime sailing time, the breeze picks up and the windjammer gets "a bone in her

teeth." As the afternoon wears on, the breeze usually begins to slacken, and by the time the anchor is dropped in a new cove, the evening calm has begun.

Once the boat is at anchor, there's often a chance to go ashore, to walk on a deserted beach, or if you're in a town, to do a little shopping. Not interested in going ashore? Perhaps you'd like to take a row or a sail in one of the smaller, accompanying boats. Dinner (or "suppa," as they say Down East) is the chance for the galley crew to really shine. It could be anything from a New England Boiled Dinner to Chicken Marbella to Spinach Lasagna—and that's just the main course.

And then there's the Lobster Bake, that windjammer tradition that everyone looks forward to—including the cook, because it's the cook's night off. The Lobster Bake, which often includes corn-on-the-cob, hamburgers, and hot dogs as well as the lobsters, is such a special part of each cruise, we've devoted a whole chapter to it.

In the evening, there's often music, stargazing, watching the phosphorescence glowing in the water, or just relaxing down below or on deck by lanternlight under the broad awning.

The Coast of Maine and the Penobscot Bay Area

Penobscot Bay is, without doubt, one of the most beautiful bodies of water in the United States, if not the world, and the best way to see it is by boat. In fact, some of the very best places in the area are accessible only by boat. For sailors, it is paradise found.

Looking east over Penobscot Bay from Camden or Rockland, the home ports of Maine's windjammer fleet, it may appear to be one solid land mass. But what you are actually seeing is almost all islands. Among the larger ones are North Haven and Vinalhaven; Little Deer Isle and Deer Isle; Isle au Haut; and, in the distance, the towering heights of Mount Desert, home to Acadia National Park.

The usual cruising grounds of the windjammers encompass all of Penobscot Bay and Blue Hill Bay from Castine in the north, to Vinalhaven and Isle au Haut in the south, to Mount Desert in the east—an area about twenty-five miles north to south and thirty-five miles east to west. While this may not seem like a large area, it has enough variety for a lifetime of sailing. There are many who sail these waters every summer and never feel the need to move farther afield.

Camden and Rockland are on the western shore of Penobscot Bay. As you look out to sea, to the west behind you are the Camden Hills with elevations of about 1,400 feet. They make great hiking and a spectacular backdrop for the setting sun when viewed from any of the islands.

Camden is a jewel-like harbor that is home to lobster boats and yachts of all types and sizes. Ashore, there are restaurants that range from haute cuisine to burgers and beer, and plenty of unique shops and places to buy souvenirs, a hat for the sun, or a sweatshirt for the breeze. Camden Hills State Park is a couple of miles east of town, and has hiking trails that provide a beautiful view over the bay.

Rockland used to be primarily a fishing harbor with all the interest and bustle that entails. In recent years, however, Rockland has rejuvenated its downtown with intriguing shops, galleries, museums and restaurants, while retaining its working waterfront—creating the best of both worlds. A lovely walk is the mile along the Rockland Breakwater that ends at the lighthouse.

Around the Bay

It's simply not possible to list all the islands, harbors, towns, and anchorages that the windjammers sail past or use to drop anchor. Working counterclockwise around the bay, starting at Camden/Rockland, here are a few of the favorites:

Gilkey Harbor—which is nestled between the larger Islesboro to the east and Seven Hundred Acre Island to the west—is a snug hideaway, home to year-round residents and summer visitors; there's a ferry to the mainland. The town of Dark Harbor has been a summer retreat for generations of prosperous New England families.

To the south are the islands of North Haven and Vinalhaven. Together they are about ten miles long, lying north to south. On the northwest coast of North Haven is Pulpit Harbor. A very narrow entrance, guarded by Pulpit Rock and seemingly no wider than a windjammer, opens into a well-protected harbor—and is a great spot to watch the sun set over the Camden Hills.

North Haven is separated from Vinalhaven by the Fox Islands Thorofare. It's a challenge to sail through, with shifting winds as well as numerous twists and turns along the four-mile passage. Halfway through the Thorofare is the pretty little town of North Haven. Busy in the summer, it's very quiet in the winter.

Vinalhaven Island, to the south, stretches down to the open Atlantic Ocean. Among the profusion of islands and ledges along the western shore is Hurricane Island, made famous by the Hurricane Island Outward Bound School. The school's "pulling boats" are a frequent sight on Penobscot Bay and Muscongus Bay to the west, as are their solitary campers roughing it on isolated islands.

The fishing town of Carvers Harbor at the southern end of the island reaches out into the ocean, and Atlantic rollers break on the rocks and ledges that lie offshore. A few miles to the east of the town is the fascinating Brimstone Island, whose beach comprises jet black stones that the sea has tumbled into smooth, rounded shapes.

On the eastern shore of Vinalhaven are the very nearly landlocked harbors of Seal Bay and Winter Harbor, which share a small entrance. Winter Harbor is long and narrow, with a prominent cliff called Starboard Rock, and Seal Bay is more open with numerous islets and anchorages. True to its name, seals do favor the bay and are frequently seen drying themselves on the ledges that are exposed at low tide.

Isle au Haut and Deer Isle

East of Vinalhaven is Isle au Haut (usually pronounced: "I'll ah Ho"). Where Vinalhaven and North Haven are set low in the water, Isle au Haut's 543-foot peak is the

LEAVE NO TRACE

The coast of Maine abounds with seals, porpoises, ospreys, eagles, and even whales. The water is cold and clear; the skies are undimmed by pollution. It may not appear to be a fragile environment, but it is.

All the vessels in the Maine Windjammer Association ascribe to the principles of the Leave No Trace Center for Outdoor Ethics. Leave No Trace promotes a code of conduct that helps protect the environment by minimizing the impact of outdoor recreation. Maine windjammer captains practiced these principles even before Leave No Trace was formalized.

The windjammers take "leave no trace" quite literally. Even after a lobster bake on the beach, the area is left just as it was found: everything that was carried in is carried out. Actually, the islands are left cleaner than they are found, because guests spend time picking up flotsam and jetsam that's been washed ashore. Most of the smaller islands in the Penobscot Bay region are privately owned but are left in their natural state. Visitors are welcome, especially if they "leave no trace."

highest point between the Camden Hills and Mount Desert. Isle au Haut has summer residents and year-round inhabitants. Both populations seem to enjoy the low-key island life. The general store on the waterfront supplies necessities, or islanders can take the ferry or—as many do—take their own boat around and past the islands of Merchants Row to Stonington, five miles away. There's a road that circumnavigates the island, giving views of Long Pond, Head Harbor, Duck Harbor, and the open ocean on the southern side. The total hike is about nine miles.

The islands of Merchants Row provide nearly limitless anchorages. Most of the islands are much less than a mile long, some only a few hundred yards. So close together are the islands that the entire area of about five miles by three miles, with its more than thirty islands, can be regarded as one big, beautiful anchorage. Crotch Island, near Stonington, is easily recognizable for its granite works, complete with tall

cranes and heavy equipment, still sporadically working away. Granite from Crotch Island was used to build the Library of Congress and Union Station in Chicago, among many other famous edifices.

Deer Isle's Stonington has a dual life as one of the lobstering centers of the Maine coast and as a longtime artists' colony. On the one hand, there are art galleries and shops; on the other is a rough and ready lobstering town with few frills. As the lobstermen say, "Paint don't catch fish." Stroll along the waterfront of Stonington and you will see how both cultures fit together.

Deer Isle and its northern appendage Little Deer Isle form the southwestern side of Eggemoggin Reach that slants northwest from Brooklin in the south to Brooksville at its northern end. Brooklin is home of *WoodenBoat* Magazine, a focus of the worldwide revival of interest in wooden boats. The "WoodenBoat Sail-In" in September is a favorite gathering of the windjammer fleet.

About midway along Eggemoggin Reach is the spidery Deer Isle Bridge, which connects Little Deer Isle to the mainland. It was built in the 1930s, but some traditionalists still grumble about changes that the bridge brought to island life. It's said that Franklin Roosevelt demanded that the bridge be high enough for his friends' large sailing yachts to be able to pass underneath.

Bucks Harbor (referred to as Buck Harbor on the chart, but to locals it's Bucks Harbor) is a favorite stopping place. Lovers of Robert McCloskey's children's book *One Morning in Maine* recognize some of the buildings in town. His island (which is still in his family) is about three miles south of Bucks Harbor near Little Deer Isle. Bucks Harbor and nearby Walker Pond were once prominent in the ice industry. Ice saws cut the "pond ice," which was then skidded and dragged by horse teams to schooners that took it south to Boston, New York City, and even the Caribbean.

Completing the counterclockwise tour of Penobscot Bay is Castine, a classic Maine town with upright white houses and picket fences. Castine is home to the Maine Maritime Academy, which owns the training ship *State of Maine* that is berthed there. Castine has a lively history. It is named after the Baron de Castine who, in the seventeenth century, allied himself with the Native Americans against the French, Dutch, and British. The British reclaimed Castine during the French and Indian War and held it during both the Revolutionary War and the War of 1812.

Blue Hill Bay and Mount Desert

To the east of Penobscot Bay are Blue Hill Bay, Swans Island, and Mount Desert. At the head of Blue Hill Bay is the town of Blue Hill, not unlike a smaller version of Camden. Swans Island has two main harbors: on the northern side is Mackerel Cove at the eastern shore of the twisty Casco Passage, and on the south is Burnt Coat Harbor—its name probably being a corruption of Burned Coast, or côte, in French. The island is named after Colonel James Swan, who fought in the Revolutionary War and later helped hatch a plot to smuggle Marie Antoinette out of Paris and bring her to Wiscasset, Maine. It didn't work, of course, and Marie Antoinette went to the guillotine.

Maine islands and ledges (reefs) are famous for their intriguing names. The origin of some names, such as Burnt Coat, can be guessed at, but many origins are lost in history (and some of the more risqué names were cleaned up during the nineteenth century). Who can help but wonder about Barney's Mistake, Fling Island, the Brown Cow, Roaring Bull Ledge, Drunkard Ledge, Lazygut Island, and Toothacher Bay?

Mount Desert Island (you will hear it pronounced both ways: like the final course of a meal or a sandy plain) is home to Acadia National Park, one of the most popular national parks in the country. In the mid-nineteenth century, wealthy vacationers began to come to Mount Desert and build vast summer "cottages," and enjoyed a glittering social life to match. But in 1947, Mount Desert was ravaged by a fire

that destroyed many of the cottages, particularly in the Bar Harbor area. Southwest Harbor is a yachting and fishing harbor, while Northeast Harbor has glamorous yachts and summer houses. Bar Harbor is very popular among summer visitors who enjoy the park and the surrounding views.

Spectacular Somes Sound near Southwest Harbor is a four-mile-long fjord with mountains on both sides that plunge down to the water. The entrance to the fjord is only four hundred yards wide. Watch for the bald eagles that are returning to this area.

This by no means exhausts the list of beautiful anchorages. We haven't even touched on Frenchboro on Long Island, lonely Matinicus Island, or Little Cranberry Island with its spectacular views of Mount Desert. You surely will find your own favorites to provide lasting memories of the incomparable coast of Maine.

The windjammers offer cruises ranging in length from weekend getaways to six-day sailing adventures, as well as three-, four-, and five-day trips. Of course, the longer trips go farther afield and guests get to explore more of the islands, harbors, and towns of the area.

MORE INFORMATION

The Maine Windjammer Association represents all twelve vessels cited in this book. The website has all the practical details about the windjammers, including their schedules and rates; contact details; what you should bring; and how to get there. For more information about the association, call (800) 807-WIND (9463) or send an e-mail to the link on the web site: www.sailmainecoast.com

Contact details for each of the windjammers are also listed at the end of each chapter in this book.

The Famous Lobster Bake

A HIGHLIGHT OF A windjammer cruise is the Lobster Bake on the beach. This meal is highly anticipated by the guests and appreciated by the galley crew—as it gets them out of the galley for the evening. There's often an air of mystery that develops around where and when the Lobster Bake will take place. Only the captain knows for sure and even he or she can't always predict the weather. What's required is a mild evening and a beautiful beach—preferably with a view of the sunset. Not to mention, lobsters, clams, hot dogs, and all the fixings!

Every windjammer does its Lobster Bake somewhat differently, but they do share some similarities. The basic ingredients are lobsters (of course), potatoes, corn-on-the-cob, and hot dogs or hamburgers. Some common additions are salads, onions, garlic, and grilled veggies. For dessert, Maine blueberry pie is a favorite.

Some of the windjammers cook the meal on a sort of metal barbeque that hangs over the side of the vessel, but most have the Bake on a beach where it takes three or four hours to complete the whole process: preparing the fire, gathering rockweed to layer between the ingredients, and steaming (not boiling) the entire meal. So, there's plenty of time for swimming, hiking, and conversation around the fire. The lobsters usually were trapped that day, sometimes acquired directly from a lobster boat—from the sea to your plate in just a few hours.

Aware of the delicate island environment, windjammer crew members bring their own firewood from the vessel; some even bring their own sticks for roasting marshmallows. And when the Lobster Bake is finished, crews leave the beach cleaner than they found it.

Do-It-Yourself Lobster Bake

There's nothing like a Lobster Bake on a Maine beach with a windjammer as a backdrop, but having your own beach (or windjammer) isn't a requirement. If you're lucky enough to live near a public beach, you usually can pull off a fine Lobster Bake with a little planning and a permit from the local fire department. You can even have a Lobster Bake in your backyard.

In the following passage, Captain Barry King of schooner *Mary Day*, shares his secrets for an authentic Maine Lobster Bake.

"Our typical lobster bake is for 36 people with up to 100 pounds of lobster, steamed in a couple of #3 wash kettles over a fire on the

beach. That may be a little more than you want to cook, so I will just list the ingredients and the order in which we layer them into the kettles. You choose your preferred ingredients and the quantities. Be careful of who you invite for supper; after boasting about our all-you-can-eat picnic, I had one young man eat 13 lobsters in a single sitting!

Maine lobster
Steamer clams or mussels
Baby red potatoes
Peeled small onions
Corn on the cob
Hot dogs
Whole bulbs of garlic
Butter
1 tide-tossed stone
Seaweed, preferably Ascophyllum

Of course, the most important ingredient in a lobster bake is time. Time to do a little beach combing, time to take a swim before supper, time to enjoy casual conversation around the fire as everything cooks. You should plan on several hours to prepare this meal. Along with the main fare, we serve at least 3 or 4 appetizers, 2 different salads, hot dogs, hamburgers, and several desserts. We gather mussels if the tide is right.

Here is how we do it:

You may want to assemble all the ingredients and do a trial fitting into the largest kettle that will fit on your stove. If you are going to do this in your kitchen, you may need several pots. If you are lucky enough to have a big kettle and are able to build a fire in your backyard, go for it. I have also had great luck with large propane burners. You can rent those along with the kettles. I have even seen one person use a metal trash can. Just make certain that your cooking vessel is clean and free of contaminants. Most importantly, you need lots of heat to generate the

necessary steam. That's right, steam. You want to steam everything, not boil it, so a cover is very important.

I put about 2–3 inches of water in the bottom of our kettles. If you don't have seawater from the pristine Maine coast nearby, then add a couple of tablespoons of salt to help raise the boiling temperature of the water.

Get the water boiling before putting in the first layer: lobster. We pull the rubber bands off the claws before we put them in headfirst. Be careful with this step. On top of the lobster add your steamers or mussels. Next come the potatoes, onions, and garlic. It is at this point that we use a thin layer of seaweed for flavor. Don't worry if you don't have a fresh source of organic seaweed nearby. It will still taste great.

Now is the time to put in the corn. We leave ours in the husk but chop off the ends to save room. On top of this we put the final ingredient, the hot dogs. We cover all of this with a clean piece of canvas (you can use foil) and lots of seaweed to help hold in the heat and steam. Seal it up as best you can and watch for the kettle to begin to boil again. Once we see steam, we generally wait for 20 minutes of good hard steaming. I place an oblong small stone (about 3 inches long) in the center of the pile of seaweed and stand it up on end. I know it is time to check on everything when the stone falls over. The hot dogs should be split open. The potatoes should be soft enough to poke a fork through easily. Make certain that the clams or mussels have opened up. The lobster meat should be firm and white inside its shell.

Now, we realize that you may not have all of these ingredients at home, but don't hesitate to create your own variation on this celebratory theme. This highlight of most windjammer cruises is a festive occasion to be shared with good friends. Of course you can always come on a cruise for a first-hand look at how we do it. By the way, how many lobsters can you eat?"

How to Eat a Lobster—and Clams and Mussels

Eating a lobster is a pretty basic experience. And pretty messy. It's best done with the fingers—so just dig in; there's no wrong way to do it.

Just about everyone who eats a lobster begins the same way: with the claws and the tail. The claws are the easiest to get at; take the lobster cracker (a seagoing nutcracker, actually), or even a rock from the beach, and crack the claw through the thickest section. Pull the meat out with a fork, your fingers, or a lobster pick (which resembles an oversized dental instrument). Dunk the meat in melted butter and pop it into your mouth.

There are also useful amounts of meat in the knuckles, between the claws and the body. These are a little harder to crack than the claws, but they are worth it.

Next comes the tail: grasp the body in one hand and the tail in the other, and twist. The tail will come away from the body. Inside the body or at the big end of the tail is the "coral" or roe, some carti-laginous material, and the green tomalley, which is the liver. Some prize the tomalley; some are concerned that this is where any pollutants concentrate. To get the meat out of the tail, take a knife, slit lengthwise the underside of the tail, and pull the meat out. Or break off the end of the tail, stick your index finger in, and push the meat out.

The little fins at the end of the tail often have a bit of meat in them, as well as some sweet juice. Break off the fins, place one between your teeth, and squeeze the meat out. This tooth-strainer method also works well for the eight little legs on each side of the body.

Lobsters with a new, soft shell are called "shedders." They have less meat and more liquid. Some believe the flavor of shedders is more delicate and that the extra liquid has a kind of poaching effect on the meat.

Clams and Mussels

Eating steamed clams ("steamers") is easier, but there is a bit of technique. The shells should have popped opened in cooking—discard any clams whose shells remain closed. Pull the clam out of the open shell, and pull the covering off the neck—that's all there is to it. Mussels don't have necks, but the same process works: discard any with unopened shells. Everything inside the opened mussels is edible, except for the little pearls that are sometimes found there.

Digging for clams requires a clam rake or a shovel, but you can gather a few with your hands. Clams usually are found between six inches and a foot under the surface of muddy flats beneath a little air hole. Wash off the clams, and let them sit for an hour or so in seawater to clean themselves. Steam them Lobster Bake-style or in a big pot of salt water.

If you want to gather your own mussels, look for those in clean, flowing water at or below the low-tide mark—you're going to have to get your feet wet. Scrape the beard (or bysuss) off the shell, and steam the mussels either Lobster Bake-style, or with white wine, chopped onions, and garlic for moules marinière.

American Eagle

IN 1930 IN GLOUCESTER, MASSACHUSETTS, *Andrew and Rosalie*, which later would be rechristened *American Eagle*, splashed into the harbor from the United Sail Loft Wharf where she had been built. She sailed ten days later on her maiden voyage. Chances are, no one present guessed this launch signaled the beginning of the end of a way of life. As it turned out, *Andrew and Rosalie* was the last fishing schooner built in Gloucester.

But, decades remained before fishing under sail was overtaken by vessels with auxiliary power, so *Andrew and Rosalie* was part of the Gloucester fishing fleet for more than fifty years, chasing swordfish during the summer and dory trawling during the winter. (Dory trawling is vividly depicted in Rudyard Kipling's novel *Captains Courageous* and in the great movie adaptation with Spencer Tracy and Freddie Bartholomew.) Typically, fishing schooners were built with an eye to speed, as the first schooner back from the fishing grounds got the best price for its catch and spoilage was minimized.

In 1941, during World War II, *Andrew and Rosalie* was renamed *American Eagle* by Ben Pine, then-owner and famous racing captain.

American Eagle continued as a fishing vessel right up until 1983. When Captain John Foss bought her in 1984, she was tied up only a few hundred yards from where she had been built half a century before. But after fifty-three years of hard use on the North Atlantic, *American Eagle* was feeling her age and was in just-good-enough condition to make it from Gloucester to Rockland, Maine, and the North End Shipyard where she underwent a complete rebuild.

Captain John notes that "it took about six months to build her the first time and two years to rebuild her." *American Eagle* was restored in the traditional manner, out of pine and oak, with double-sawn frames and beautiful wood-paneled cabins down below. She has a reliable inboard engine, enabling her to go farther afield than schooners powered by only the traditional yawl boats. So although the *Eagle* now looks and feels like a new and well-maintained vessel, her complete overhaul honored the traditions of her original builders. In fact, you still can see some of the original timbers and planks. For example, some of the ceiling (the inside planking) of the fish hold still shows the pockmarks made by the pitchforks used to unload the catch.

29

TOP: *American Eagle* slips along in a light breeze.

ABOVE: Captain John Foss.

What Captain John doesn't know about sailing the Maine coast probably isn't worth knowing. He has been sailing the Maine coast since he was a boy and worked on several windjammers as a summer job while in college. He took his sailing experience to sea as a deck officer in the U.S. Coast Guard from 1969 to 1973. After which, he bought and rebuilt *Lewis R. French*, which was 103 years old when Captain John motored her down from Eastport, Maine, to Rockland for restoration. In winter, Captain John can still be found working on old boats and vessels at the North End Shipyard. His encyclopedic knowledge of the Maine coast, its wildlife, and its history is a hallmark of any trip aboard the *American Eagle*.

American Eagle is a big, stable vessel built for the challenges of fishing the North Atlantic offshore in summer and winter. She is ninety-two feet on deck with a beam of twenty feet and a deep draft of eleven feet, six inches. As a fishing schooner, the *Eagle* could carry one hundred thousand pounds of fish; now she carries twenty-six passengers and six crew.

John has co-owned the North End Shipyard with Captains Doug and Linda Lee since 1973. It is here that most schooners in the Maine windjammer fleet are hauled and inspected. The *Eagle* is always kept in ready condition; as one of the few boats in the fleet licensed for international waters, her cruises take passengers to the coastal waters of Canada as well as to tall-ship events in Boston, Massachusetts, and New York City. A few months after her relaunch in 1986, the *Eagle* took part in New York's Parade of Sail, celebrating the rededication of the Statue of Liberty. As a testament to her proud heritage and John's careful stewardship, the *American Eagle* was designated a National Historic Landmark in 1991.

Maine coastal cruises run three, four, or six days, with the Canadian cruises typically running between eight and fourteen days. Through the years, the *Eagle* has ventured as far east as Lunenburg, Nova Scotia, and as far west as New York Harbor. Her windward sailing ability, auxiliary diesel engine, and hydraulic anchor windlass are helpful on these longer cruises.

Cruises to New Brunswick and the Bay of Fundy are memorable ones. Sailing east of Mount Desert Island, you may drop anchor at beautiful Great Wass Island, Roque Island, Passamaquoddy Bay, or Campobello Island, Franklin Roosevelt's summer retreat. These destinations—as well as Grand Manan Island and the reversing falls on the St. John River—are distant goals for many sailors, and anyone who has reached these locations by sea will inevitably return with a few stories to tell. Once past Mount Desert, you begin to leave the tourist world behind; pleasure boats give way to working fishing fleets, fog lingers on fir-lined shores, and the adventures begin.

Closer to home, one of Captain John's favorite harbors is snug Pulpit Harbor (the entrance to which has long been marked by an osprey's nest atop a rocky outcropping). Or you may drop anchor in one of the many coves of the dozens of islands in Merchants Row (south of Deer Isle and just north of spectacular Isle au Haut with its high hills and excellent walking trails). John believes the best cruise doesn't have an itinerary and the destination each day is decided by whim, wind, and weather.

Captain John refers to the cooking on *American Eagle* as "high-end comfort food." All the cooking is done on a woodstove; refrigeration is provided by two iceboxes: one for the galley, and one for the guests. The cook makes every effort to get the best and freshest food—bought locally. The menu is varied and innovative and is well received by the many returning guests who come for the sailing, the food, the scenery, and the captain's stories. The cooks are also adept at accommodating special diets with advance notice. Baking is done aboard, usually early in the day, although bread hot from the oven often accompanies dinner on deck. Every cruise has a Lobster Bake on the beach, with the captain at the campfire, serving a little white wine and brewing his bracing, old-fashioned campfire coffee to go with pie to top off the feast.

Hand-churned ice cream in a variety of flavors is a regular feature of the menu, along with a delectable array of fresh-baked pastries and cookies, not to mention the *Eagle*'s famous brownies. Specialties of the galley include hearty soups, fresh fish, and roasts.

After dinner, Captain John is apt to treat you to a seafaring story or two as you're lulled by the gentle lapping of the waves on the hull. Be sure to take a last look at the sky before going below. Chances are, you've never seen so many stars. Want help identifying them? Just ask the captain.

TOP: Guests and crew raise the mainsail.

ABOVE: A calm day on Penobscot Bay.

BELOW: The *American Eagle* catches a good sailing breeze.

American Eagle

Captain John Foss
Length on deck: 92 feet
Length overall: 125 feet
Guests: 26
(207) 594-8007
(800) 648-4544
info@schooneramericaneagle.com
www.schooneramericaneagle.com

American Eagle   31

Quesadillas

This Tex-Mex favorite pairs nicely with the *American Eagle*'s Black Bean Soup.

2 boneless chicken breasts, about 6 ounces each

4 tablespoons olive oil

1 teaspoon minced fresh cilantro

Salt and pepper

8 soft corn tortillas

1 cup prepared salsa

1 cup shredded cheddar cheese

SERVES 4

Cut the chicken lengthwise into thin strips (about 6 strips per breast). Toss the strips with 2 tablespoons of the olive oil, the cilantro, and a little salt and pepper, and marinate for about 10 minutes.

Preheat the oven to 350 degrees. In a skillet, heat the remaining oil over medium-high heat and sauté the chicken until it is golden brown and just cooked through, turning each piece as needed to brown evenly. Remove to a plate and set aside.

Lay 4 of the tortillas out on the counter and spread 2 tablespoons of salsa over each one. Lay 3 strips of chicken over each tortilla. Sprinkle about ¼ cup of cheese over each tortilla.

Lay the remaining tortillas out on the counter, spread 2 tablespoons of salsa over each one, and place over the filled tortillas. Transfer to a baking sheet, cover with parchment paper and bake 10–12 minutes, until the quesadillas are lightly toasted and the cheese is melted. Cut into wedges and serve warm.

Cucumber Salad

This crunchy salad is a perfect summer side dish.
Feel free to use light sour cream if you prefer.

Combine all of the ingredients in a bowl
and mix well. Chill before serving.

2 cups very thinly sliced
  European cucumber

½ cup very thinly sliced
  onion

½ cup sour cream

2 tablespoons white wine
  vinegar

1 tablespoon minced
  fresh dill

Salt and black pepper,
  to taste

SERVES 4

Black Bean Soup

1 ham hock

½ pound dried black beans

1 teaspoon liquid smoke

1 cup diced onion

1 cup diced green
   pepper

1 cup diced red pepper

1 teaspoon cayenne
   pepper, or to taste

Salt and black pepper,
   to taste

SERVES 4-6

This hearty soup is perfect for a cool day on deck.
Cayenne gives it heat, but you can adjust the
amount to suit your tastes.

In a large pot, cover the ham hock with 2 ½ quarts of cold water. Bring to a boil, then reduce heat and simmer for 1 hour.

Add the black beans and the liquid smoke. Bring to a boil, then reduce heat and simmer for 1–2 hours, or until beans begin to soften.

Remove the ham hock from the soup and let it sit until it is cool enough to handle. Pull the meat from the bones, breaking or chopping it into bite-sized pieces. Add the meat back to the soup, along with the onions, peppers, and cayenne and simmer for another hour or so, or until the beans are completely tender. When beans are quite soft, use a potato masher to break up some of the beans. Season with salt and black pepper. Serve with a dollop of sour cream, accompanied by Chicken Quesadillas and Cucumber Salad.

Scallop and Shrimp Kabobs with Tri-Colored Cous Cous

12 large sea scallops

12 large shrimp

¼ cup soy-ginger sauce

8 chunks green pepper

8 chunks red pepper

8 chunks red onion

4 bamboo skewers, soaked
    overnight in water

1 package tri-colored
    cous cous

Lemon slices and minced
    parsley, for garnish

SERVES 4

SOY-GINGER SAUCE

½ cup soy sauce

½ cup sesame oil

½ cup rice vinegar

¼ cup honey

1 thumb-sized chunk fresh
    ginger, peeled and
    chopped, or more to
    taste

6 cloves garlic, peeled

MAKES ABOUT 2 CUPS

Native sea scallops are the star of the show in this colorful seafood favorite. The cook aboard the *American Eagle* makes his own gingery soy sauce, but you could use store bought if you are short of time.

Preheat the oven to 425 degrees. Toss the scallops and shrimp with the soy ginger sauce and marinate for about 10 minutes.

Place 3 scallops, 3 shrimp, and 2 chunks of each vegetable on a skewer, alternating the shellfish and the vegetables as you place them on the skewer.

Place on a lightly greased baking sheet or roasting pan and bake at 425 degrees for 15–18 minutes, until the vegetables are tender and the shellfish is just cooked through.

While kabobs are baking, prepare the cous cous according to package instructions. Spread the prepared cous cous onto a platter.

Arrange the finished kabobs over the cous cous. Garnish with minced parsley and slices of fresh lemon.

Soy-Ginger Sauce

Combine all ingredients in a blender and blend until smooth. Strain through a mesh strainer. Will keep, refrigerated, indefinitely.

Oops-I-Broke-the-Cake Trifle

You can spice this up by drizzling coffee brandy over the crumbled cake as you layer the ingredients.
Top with sliced strawberries or shaved chocolate—or both.

Combine the pudding mix with the whipping cream and whip until stiff peaks form.

In the bottom of a clear glass bowl, place ⅓ of the cake crumbles. Spread ⅓ of the pudding mixture over the cake. Sprinkle ⅓ of the toffee chips over the pudding mixture. Repeat with remaining ingredients.

Spread the whipped cream over the top.

2 boxes instant cheese cake pudding

2 pints whipping cream

1 9-inch chocolate cake, crumbled

1 package (8 ounces) toffee chips

2 cups whipped cream

SERVES 6-8

Angelique

ANGELIQUE IS A DISTINCTIVE VESSEL: her dark red (or tanbark) sails, plumb bow, and ketch rig make her instantly recognizable, even from a distance. She is a stunning sight set against the blue water and dark green islands of Penobscot Bay. *Angelique* has been owned and operated by Captain Mike McHenry and his wife Lynne since 1986. Their children, Ryan and Katie Rose, virtually grew up aboard and are helping out as crew aboard today.

Angelique is designed after the fishing trawlers of the southwest coast of England—fast, strong sailing vessels that plied the rough waters in the late 1800s. *Angelique*'s tanbark sails are traditional, as is her ketch rig. She was built in 1980 to carry passengers.

Angelique's well-thought-out design takes advantage of modern conveniences where they are best suited. Two powerful diesel engines push her along when the wind dies. *Angelique* has seven watertight compartments for safety and state-of-the-art electronics for navigation and communication. While her design echoes the beauty of the trawlers of the 1800s, her amenities provide guests with a far more comfortable experience than they would have had in the nineteenth century.

Guests appreciate *Angelique*'s deckhouse salon, complete with a piano—a cozy area to relax without going below. With lots of windows, a pot-bellied stove, and easy access to the galley, the deck salon is a great place to watch the scenery slide by, away from the breeze or sun, and to gather in the evening for music and conversation. The salon is also a handy place to stow jackets or hats, saving a trip below to your cabin. The well-ventilated cabins are wood paneled, and each has a freshwater sink and a reading light over each bunk, as well as plenty of fresh linens and towels.

As with all vessels, *Angelique* requires constant loving attention. When we were on board in November, after the sailing season, the crew—including Captain Mike—was laying a new fir deck and getting *Angelique* battened down for winter. In early spring, painting, varnishing, and preparation for the new season begins again.

Uninhabited islands, small fishing villages, mountains, and deep bays define the Maine coast experience. Chances are you will see seals, porpoises, eagles, ospreys, and even some puffins. *Angelique* runs a number of cruises with a guest naturalist aboard to help spot and identify wildlife,

ABOVE: A view of the foredeck from the rigging.

BELOW: Preparing to row ashore.

including trips out to remote Mount Desert Rock and Schoodic Ridge. Watercolor, lighthouse, and whale watching cruises are popular choices.

Guests often are amazed at how dark and quiet evenings are on the coast of Maine. Seeing how brightly the stars shine, away from the glare of city lights, is often a revelation to guests who haven't been aboard before. Lynne loves the stillness of the night after the breeze has dropped and the tiny points of bioluminescence appear—like marine fireflies that move mysteriously about in the water below. In August everyone looks forward to the Perseid meteor showers. Guests may be treated to the spectacular display of the aurora borealis, also known as the northern lights, in the fall.

Angelique's cruising grounds are between Boothbay Harbor and Mount Desert (home of Acadia National Park). Some of *Angelique*'s favorite anchorages are Buck's Harbor and Little Cranberry Island (both great places for a brisk walk or leisurely stroll ashore) and Holbrook Island and the Little Thorofare.

Cooking on a windjammer is like cooking for a very large family. Meals range from semi-gourmet to homey favorites, and all focus on healthy choices using the freshest ingredients possible. *Angelique*'s galley is in a great location: forward in the deckhouse, which allows the galley crew to see what's going on while preparing meals. Guests appreciate this location, too, as they can tuck inside and talk with the cooks, watch what's happening on deck, or even help out if so inclined.

Angelique's meals are cooked on and baked in a kerosene-fired Dickenson Beaufort stove that was built for shipboard use. This stove does not have burners but rather a large, flat heated stovetop; it's a constant shifting of pots and pans to learn where the hot and cool spots are.

Guests frequently ask for the recipes so they can make their on-board favorites at home. *Angelique*'s New England Boiled Dinner is a particular favorite. The captain and cook credit the success of their boiled dinners to the quality of the corned beef locally available. This meal simmers gently throughout the day, filling the deckhouse with an incredible aroma, making it hard to wait for the dinner bell to ring. Brownies—made with unsweetened chocolate squares, chocolate chips, and chocolate syrup—also are a favorite. In fact, one guest returned saying "I came back for the brownies; you better be making them!" as she boarded.

One may ask, "What's a typical day like in the galley?" Well, it begins early. The cook is the first to rise, lights the stove and begins planning for the day. Galley assis-

tants are up and about shortly after.

A coffee tray appears on deck at 7:00 a.m. every morning, and breakfast is served at 8:00 a.m. Shortly after breakfast, guests and crew are often seen on deck helping with food preparation: peeling potatoes, chopping onions or slicing strawberries for the meals to follow. Lunch is served on deck while underway, weather permitting, and dinner is around 6:00 p.m. Dessert is served afterwards, just in time to watch the sunset.

Angelique's menu has changed with the times, with new dishes added to the list of old favorites. To this day, returning guests ask for their favorites, some of which have been on the menu for twenty years. Special diets can be accommodated when ample notice is provided. It's amazing to see what can be prepared in the galley; limited space and ever-changing conditions with wind

and weather can be a challenge. But guests always seem to find a "favorite," whether it's a special anchorage, a place on deck, or a recipe, as they are introduced to the *Angelique* windjamming experience.

ABOVE: Furling sails on *Angelique*'s bowsprit.

BELOW: *Angelique* shows her speed.

Angelique

Captain Mike McHenry
Length on deck: 95 feet
Length overall: 130 feet
Beam: 24 1/2 feet
Draft: 11 feet
Sail area: 5,300 square feet
Guests: 29
(800) 282-9989
www.sailangelique.com

Cheddar Broccoli Soup

4 tablespoons butter

1 cup diced onion

⅓ cup flour

3 ½ cups chicken broth

2 cups milk

½ teaspoon garlic powder

2 cups shredded cheddar
cheese

6 slices American cheese

4 cups bite-sized broccoli
florets, blanched

Salt and black pepper, to
taste

Bacon bits and croutons,
for garnish

SERVES 4-6

This rich soup is a perfect lunch dish for a cool day on deck.

In a large pot over medium heat, melt the butter until it begins to sizzle. Add the onions and sauté until translucent, about 5 minutes. Stir in the flour and cook 2–3 minutes, stirring frequently.

Whisk in the chicken broth, milk, and garlic powder. Bring to a boil, stirring constantly, then reduce heat and simmer 5 minutes.

Stir in the cheeses and broccoli and cook 5–10 minutes longer, until the cheese is melted and the soup is hot. Season to taste with the salt and black pepper. Serve with bacon bits and croutons.

Mexican Lasagna

This recipe layers traditional Tex-Mex ingredients and is served hot and bubbling from the oven.

Preheat the oven to 350 degrees. In a large bowl, combine the chicken, cheddar, pepper jack, scallions, sour cream, chilies, cumin, salt, and black pepper. Mix well.

Lightly grease an 8×8-inch square or 8-inch round casserole pan. Spread about ¼ cup of salsa over the bottom. Place 1 tortilla over the salsa and spread half of the chicken mixture over the tortilla.

Top with 3 more tortillas, spreading about 2 tablespoons of the salsa between each tortilla.

Spread the remaining chicken mixture over the tortilla and top with 3 more tortillas, spreading about 2 tablespoons of salsa between the tortillas.

Top with the remaining salsa, Monterey jack cheese, and olives if you are using.

Bake at 350 for 45–50 minutes, until bubbling and lightly browned on top. Let set 10 minutes before serving.

3 cups cooked shredded or diced chicken

¾ cup shredded sharp cheddar cheese

¼ cup pepper jack cheese

¾ cup sliced scallions

1 cup sour cream

½ cup diced mild green chilies, such as Poblano

1 teaspoon cumin

Salt and black pepper, to taste

2 cups mild or medium salsa

7 flour tortillas, 8 inches round

½ cup Monterey jack cheese, for topping

½ cup sliced black olives (optional)

SERVES 4-6

Cole Slaw

2 cups shredded red cabbage

4 cups shredded green cabbage

2 tablespoons vinegar

1 tablespoon sugar

½ cup sour cream or yogurt, more if needed

½ cup mayonnaise, more if needed

Dash of your favorite seasonings, such as cayenne, mustard powder, celery seed, paprika, caraway seed, garlic powder, etc.

Salt and pepper to taste

SERVES 4-6

This creamy slaw is a simple and versatile side dish. It's great with sandwiches or grilled fish or chicken.

In a large bowl combine the cabbage, vinegar, sugar, sour cream, and mayonnaise and mix well. Add additional sour cream and/or mayonnaise if you would like it creamier. Add spices, salt, and pepper, to taste.

Cottage Cheese Dill Bread

This fabulous moist bread is a passenger favorite aboard *Angelique*.

Sprinkle the yeast over the water in a medium bowl. Stir in 1 teaspoon of the honey and set aside.

In a separate bowl, whisk together the cottage cheese, onion, dill, baking powder, salt, egg, and remainder of honey or sugar.

Stir the cottage cheese mixture into yeast mixture and mix well. Add the flour and mix to create a dough. Turn out onto a lightly floured surface and knead for 2 or 3 minutes, adding flour if necessary to create a dough that will be firm but somewhat sticky. Place in a greased bowl, cover with a damp cloth, and let rise for about an hour or until doubled in size.

When dough has doubled in size, move onto a lightly floured surface and knead for 2 or 3 minutes. Form into a loaf shape and place in a greased 9×5×2½-inch loaf pan. Let rise until doubled in size, about 1–1½ hours.

Preheat oven to 350 degrees and bake the loaf for 40–45 minutes, until golden brown. Bread should spring back when pressed. Cool for 10 minutes in the pan, then run a knife around the edge of the pan and remove the loaf to a rack to cool completely.

1 ½ teaspoons yeast

¼ cup warm water

4 teaspoons honey or sugar

1 cup cottage cheese, creamed in a food processor or mashed with a potato masher

1 tablespoon shredded raw onion

1 tablespoon minced fresh dill (or 1 teaspoon dry dill weed)

½ teaspoon baking powder

¼ teaspoon salt

1 egg

2 ¼ cups flour, more if needed

MAKES 1 LOAF

Brownies

These classic bars just seem to disappear as soon as they come out of the oven.

3 ounces unsweetened chocolate

½ cup butter

3 eggs

1 ½ cups sugar

1 teaspoon vanilla

1 cup flour

2 tablespoons chocolate syrup

1 cup semisweet chocolate chips

1 ¼ cups walnuts

MAKES 4-5 DOZEN

Preheat oven to 325 degrees. Grease a 9×13-inch baking pan. In a saucepan over low heat, melt together the chocolate and butter. In a separate bowl beat together the eggs and sugar until light and thick. Stir in the vanilla.

Add the melted chocolate mixture to the egg mixture. Stir in the flour, chocolate syrup, chocolate chips, and walnuts. Pour into the prepared pan and bake at 325 degrees for 25–30 minutes, until set. Cool completely before cutting into squares.

Grace Bailey

GRACE BAILEY IS THE OLDEST of Ann and Ray Williamson's three green schooners berthed in Camden, Maine. Built in Patchogue, New York, by master shipwright Oliver Perry, the *Grace Bailey* dates back to 1882 and was the namesake of first owner Edwin Bailey's daughter. The ship was a hard-working, cargo-carrying coasting schooner for the next sixty years, plying the waters laden with granite, lumber, ice, and other freight. She ventured as far afield as South Carolina, Georgia, and even the Caribbean, carrying fruit as part of the burgeoning trade between the U.S. mainland and the islands. (Today, *Grace Bailey* is one of only four surviving historic coasters—ships specifically designed to carry cargo along the coast—that are currently operating out of Maine ports of call; the other three are *Mercantile*, which also is owned by the Williamsons, and two more members of the Maine windjammer fleet: *Stephen Taber* and *Lewis R. French*.)

In 1906, Edwin—apparently much taken with his granddaughter, Martha—rechristened *Grace Bailey* as *Mattie*, using Martha's pet name. In 1919, *Mattie* was sold to Captain Herbert Black of Brooksville, Maine. She became a Maine coasting schooner carrying general cargo, including a notable shipment of local granite that would become part of the New York City Post Office. She remained *Mattie*, although her vocation changed during the years, until the Williamsons rebuilt her in 1990, when she again became *Grace Bailey*.

If you were standing just about anywhere along America's inhabited coastline during the late 1800s, you wouldn't have looked twice at the graceful schooners coming and going, loading and unloading cargo, any more than today we would remark on an eighteen-wheeler on the highway. According to *Grace Bailey*'s nomination for National Historic Landmark status: "Tens of thousands of these vessels were built and operated on the Pacific, Atlantic and Gulf coasts, and on the Great Lakes in the 19th and early 20th centuries. The 'freight trucks' of their time, the coasting schooners carried coal, bricks, iron ore, grain, oysters, and numerous other bulk product between ports."

In 1939, her cargo changed, and she became a passenger schooner under the charge of Captain Frank Swift, who is credited with originating the windjammer passenger trade. Captain Frank saw two opportunities: to let the public experience the romance of cruising under sail and to

sleeping bags in the boat shop. His work crew included a dozen ship's carpenters, and together they began to dismantle the 123-foot schooner plank by plank. Some of the features that had survived through the years—such as the beautiful hand-carved paneling found below decks—were restored and reinstalled. The schooner had begun anew, and it seemed a good time to celebrate her new lease on life by rechristening her *Grace Bailey*. The restored main cabin even contains a piano, just as it did in earlier days.

This devotion to authenticity is part and parcel of the Williamsons' love for their schooners. Still meticulously maintained, the three schooners in the little fleet are tied in the inner harbor in Camden, busily loading and unloading passengers early summer through September, and lying quietly alongside the dock under their canvas covers during the winter months.

After Ann and Ray bought their small fleet, they finally were able to sail together as a family. At this time, their daughters were age six and three and a half. From this time on, the Williamsons would sail as a family. Having been a teacher for most of her working life, Ann started her first summer as a deckhand, hoping to learn the ropes. She soon became a competent sailor, all the while caring for two small children. As Ann says in her cookbook: "It became obvious that I was needed more in the galley. The system of ordering provisions was costly with the cook on each boat doing her own ordering. I figured out the best places to buy meat, fish, and produce; dry goods and paper products, to supply all the boats."

With the same can-do spirit that led her to jump aboard as a deckhand so the family could sail together, Ann set about learning

ABOVE: Captain Ray and Ann Williamson and their daughters Allysa and Kristi.

preserve these historic vessels, as rail and over-the-road transport began to put an end to their useful lives as cargo vessels.

Captain Ray had been working for the previous owners of the three green schooners, and he and Ann knew that someday they wanted their own vessel. When *Mistress*, *Mercantile*, and *Mattie* were put up for sale as a group, Ray and Ann took the plunge, even though they never imagined owning all three.

For the first two years, Ray and Ann operated all three boats, but Ray had become something of an expert on the care and feeding of historic vessels. After extensive work on the *Mercantile* during the first two winters, the Williamsons undertook a complete restoration of the *Mattie*. Anyone who had sailed the Maine coast before 1990 might recognize today's rebuilt *Grace Bailey* as the former *Mattie*. But one might also miss the resemblance.

The restoration meant sixteen-hour days for Ray, with Ann and their two girls often joining him after school, curling up in the ropes in the galley, working as cook for the first three seasons on *Mercantile*. Ann was able to bring economies of scale to bear in provisioning and preparing meals aboard each vessel. Often guests would lend a hand or just moral support. There were recipes and menus that had been prepared by the ship's cooks before the Williamsons bought the three schooners, but Ann soon developed a repertoire of her own that guests loved. Some even shared their own recipes, which are in use on the green schooners to this day.

Eventually, Ray and Ann's daughters were able to lend a hand above and below deck. Allysa loved to make breads and pie crusts; Kristi loved preparing desserts. Ann cooked aboard the *Grace Bailey* for fourteen seasons—rising at 4:30 a.m. to light the woodstove and finishing the day's labors at around 7:00 p.m. This is what Ann refers to as her "summer vacation," after which she would return to her job as a kindergarten teacher in the Camden school system.

Ann still has an active role in the galley, although she no longer cooks aboard. She still manages the galleys on each vessel, ordering provisions, planning menus, training cooks, and sometimes filling in for a cruise here and there when needed.

As with *Mercantile* and *Mistress*, guests aboard *Grace Bailey* are treated to the signature Captain's Barbeque, or, on shorter or weekend cruises, the Surf and Turf that combines the best of the lobster feast with the Captain's Barbeque. Ray says he always had a vision of having a good, old-fashioned barbeque with a grill set out over the rail where he could cook steaks, ribs, and chicken for his guests. He jokes, "I always thought it would be good for business to anchor upwind of the rest of the windjammer fleet and [let] the smells of our barbeque drift down!"

As the oldest of the Williamsons' green schooners, *Grace Bailey* has a special place in their hearts, and Ray still captains her himself.

TOP: Steering on a calm day.

ABOVE: Rebuilding *Grace Bailey*.

LEFT: *Grace Bailey*, under way with speed and stability.

Grace Bailey

Captain Ray and Ann Williamson
Length on deck: 81 feet
Length overall: 123 feet
Guests: 29
(207) 236-2938
(800) 736-7981
sail@mainewindjammercruises.com
www.mainewindjammercruises.com

Guacamole

This classic dip makes great use of summer's ripe tomatoes. Fresh lemon juice and garlic give this favorite a nice kick.

3 large, ripe avocados, pitted

½ cup finely chopped onion

3 cloves garlic, minced

1 cup chopped tomato

2 teaspoons fresh lemon juice

Salt and black pepper, to taste

SERVES 6-8

Scoop the avocados out of their skins with a spoon and mash in a bowl with a potato masher.

Add the onion, garlic, tomato, and lemon juice and mix well. Season to taste with salt. Serve with tortilla chips.

Garden Beet Salad

1 tablespoon red wine vinegar

2 teaspoons vegetable oil

2 teaspoons brown sugar

1 teaspoon Dijon mustard

¼ teaspoon salt

Pinch of ground cloves

1 can sliced beets, or 2 cups
   cooked sliced beets

½ head iceberg lettuce,
   washed and torn into bite-
   sized pieces

½ head of Romaine, washed
   and torn into bite-sized
   pieces

½ cup diced cucumber

SERVES 4-6

Try roasting fresh scrubbed beets in a 375 degree oven until easily pierced with a fork—45 minutes to an hour. The skins will peel off easily after roasting.

In a medium bowl, whisk together vinegar, oil, brown sugar, mustard, salt, and cloves. Add sliced beets and toss gently to coat. Chill for 1 hour.

Just before serving, toss lettuce in a large salad bowl with the marinated beets. Sprinkle cucumber over the top and serve immediately.

Steamed Brown Bread

Passengers really enjoy eating brown bread when it is nice and warm, especially after seeing it cooked on top of the stove in coffee cans!

Grease a 1-pound coffee can. In a small bowl, pour boiling water over the raisins. Let sit 2–3 minutes, until plumped. Drain and set aside.

In a large bowl, whisk together the dry ingredients. Whisk in the buttermilk and molasses, stirring until smooth. Add the raisins and stir to combine. Pour the batter into the prepared coffee can and cover tightly with foil. Tie a piece of kitchen twine around the can to secure the foil. Place the filled can in a deep pot with a tightly fitting lid.

Bring a kettle of water to a boil and pour enough boiling water into the pot to come one quarter of the way up the side of the can. Cover the pot and steam over low to medium heat for 3–4 hours, replenishing water as needed to remain at least one quarter of the way up the side of the can (the water should remain at barely a simmer). When a knife inserted into the center of the bread comes out clean, remove from the pot and allow to cool, in the can, for 10 minutes. Run a knife around the edge of the bread and gently shake the bread loose from the can. Slice into rounds and serve warm with butter.

⅓ cup raisins

1 cup boiling water

⅓ cup cornmeal

⅓ cup flour

⅓ cup whole wheat flour

¾ teaspoon baking soda

½ teaspoon salt

⅔ cups buttermilk

¼ cup molasses

MAKES 1 LOAF

Captain's Barbeque

It's always a fun meal when Captain Ray cooks on deck and gets to enjoy the company of the passengers. He usually grills marinated vegetables as well.

1 rack baby back ribs (8 ribs)

8 chicken drumsticks

3 each twelve-ounce sirloin steaks, halved

About 2 ½ cups Souvlaki Marinade (see recipe, or use your favorite barbeque sauce)

Salt and pepper, to taste

SERVES 6-8

SOUVLAKI MARINADE

1 cup olive oil

1 cup lemon juice

½ cup minced garlic

2 tablespoons dried thyme

1 tablespoon dried basil

MAKES 2½ CUPS

Preheat the oven to 350 degrees. Bake the drumsticks in a baking dish for 30 minutes, then set aside to cool.

In a large pot cover the ribs with water, bring to a boil, then simmer for 20 minutes. Drain and set aside to cool.

Lay the steaks in a non-reactive casserole pan or bowl and cover with ½ cup of the Souvlaki Marinade. Lay the drumsticks over the steaks and cover with an additional ½ cup of marinade or sauce. Lay the ribs on top and cover with an additional ½ cup of marinade or sauce. Place in the refrigerator to marinate for 2 hours.

Remove all of the meats from the marinade and season with salt and pepper on all sides. Grill the drumsticks and ribs until caramelized on the outside, heated through and falling off the bone. Grill the steaks to desired doneness. Use the remaining ½ cup of marinade to baste all of the meat as it is grilling.

Souvlaki Marinade

Mix all of the ingredients together.

Chocolate Zucchini Cake

**This is a very light, delicious cake.
No one can believe it has fresh zucchini in it!**

Preheat the oven to 350 degrees.
Grease a 9×13-inch baking pan.
Sift together the flour, baking powder,
baking soda, and salt. Set aside.

In a saucepan over medium-low heat,
melt together the chocolate and vegetable oil. Remove from heat.

Blend in the sugar. Stir in the vanilla,
then beat in the eggs, one at a time.

Stir the flour mixture into the chocolate mixture, mixing just until smooth.
Stir in the zucchini.

Pour into the prepared pan and bake
for 35 minutes, or until a toothpick
inserted in the center comes out clean.
Sprinkle with confectioner's sugar or
frost with chocolate frosting.

2 ounces unsweetened
  chocolate

¾ cup vegetable oil

1 ½ cups sugar

½ teaspoon vanilla

2 eggs

1 ½ cups flour

¾ teaspoon baking powder

½ teaspoon baking soda

½ teaspoon salt

1 ½ cups shredded zucchini

SERVES 6-8

Heritage

DOUG AND LINDA LEE are the owners and co-captains of *Heritage*, the only schooner in the Maine windjammer fleet that was designed and built by her captains. *Heritage* celebrated her twenty-fifth sailing season in 2007, and Doug proudly states, "This vessel has never left the dock without us."

Since they were young, the Captains Lee have been interested in sailing vessels, but their interest laid more in commercial sailing than in yachting. The couple began as deckhands and galleymates, gamely taking on any job aboard. Through the years, they learned the ins and outs of the trade. As Captain Doug says, "We jumped in with both feet." Doug and Linda had already rebuilt and were sailing their first windjammer by their mid-twenties. That was the beginning of a lifetime love affair with tall ships and the Maine coast. Both have Coast Guard master licenses; Linda is the first woman in the fleet to earn the qualification.

Having sailed their first schooner for five seasons, Doug and Linda decided they wanted a bigger vessel but couldn't find the right type and size for their needs. So they decided to do the unthinkable and build their own vessel from scratch. It's not surprising that the Lees embarked on the massive undertaking of creating their per-fect vessel from the keel up. Doug holds a master's degree in mechanical engineering and was wrapped up in the world of schooners even in college. For his senior project, he calculated the stability of coasting schooners to prove they would pass the Coast Guard design requirements in effect at the time.

Between the 1978 and 1979 sailing seasons, the Lees drew up plans for *Heritage*. The design echoed the beauty and nobility of the nineteenth-century coasting schooners that carried cargoes of bricks, lumber, coal, granite, or ice—in short, whatever needed to be transported up and down the coast before the advent of the internal combustion engine. As Captain Linda says, "Seeing the schooner with all her sails set takes your breath away." The couple's years aboard historic vessels provided insight into creating what Doug and Linda viewed as the ideal passenger schooner. *Heritage* is a big, powerful, traditionally built wooden vessel: 165 tons, 145 feet overall, 95 feet over the deck, and 24 feet wide, drawing just 8 feet of water, 18 with the centerboard down.

After a winter of planning and four years of construction at their North End Shipyard in Rockland, Maine, *Heritage* was

TOP: *Heritage* headed for a quiet anchorage.

ABOVE: Flags flying on a lovely day.

launched in 1983. *Heritage* is the newest schooner in the windjammer fleet and is described by her owners as "the next generation" of an authentic coasting schooner. Doug says: "We came to this from the point of view of amateur historians. Our interest in the maritime history of coastal Maine was the foundation of *Heritage*'s design." There were definite advantages in building their own vessel. The airy galley/dining area with large skylights and hanging plants is designed with passenger comfort in mind. Wide stairways with banisters rather than ladders provide easy access to the lower deck with generous headroom everywhere. The well-ventilated, cozy cabins have electric lighting, including reading lights over each bunk; a household receptacle for charging cell phones or cameras; and a sink with hot and cold running water. There's a freshwater shower on deck with plenty of hot water. There also are three enclosed marine heads (toilets) on deck. When at anchor, three rowboats, one with a sail, are available for exploring harbors.

Heritage is a pure sailing vessel, without an inboard engine, and is pushed along by a traditional yawl boat when the wind

lightens. The authentic 1921 "donkey" engine on deck helps to hoist the anchor and raise the sails. With the most current Coast Guard safety factors built in, *Heritage* is stable, comfortable, beautiful—and fast. She has been the overall winner of the Great Schooner Race three times and winner of her class even more often.

Heritage may be the newest vessel in the fleet, but Doug describes her as "steeped in maritime history." In fact, you'd be hard pressed to find someone who knows more about the maritime history of the Maine coast than the Lees. Anyone with an interest in the past will find Doug and Linda a wealth of information. Sailing toward Mount Desert Island, guests may learn that its first sighting by Europeans was recorded in 1604 by Samuel de Champlain, the French explorer and navigator. Captain Doug is known for his tales of the Maine coast—some factual and others, well . . . let's just say he's a good storyteller. Captain Linda is an avid amateur astronomer who loves to point out stars and constellations as night falls. The Lees' popular Coastal Maritime History and Star-Filled Night Cruises allow the captains to share their interests with their guests.

Captain Linda has always been innovative when it comes to the food served aboard, moving away from prepared mixes and store-bought bread used in the early days of windjammer cruises, and instead preparing everything from scratch. In fact, she has developed most of the recipes used on board. Building nutritious soups, adding whole grains to breads, and incorporating fresh Maine blueberries into recipes are ways she has improved the quality of schooner fare. An abundant supply of fresh fruits and vegetables is served every day. Olive, corn, and canola oils are used when sautéing vegetables for soups, and when baking breads and cakes. Special dietary needs are taken in stride. Soy milk is substituted for guests who are lactose intolerant. Lowering the sodium content of a dish is never a problem because herbs are used for seasoning instead of salt.

The cook and two assistants, one known as the "cookie cook," make up the galley crew. Many kinds of bread are baked in the wood-burning Shipmate cookstove, and as many as ten loaves and six pies may be turned out in a day. The fresh herbs used for seasoning soups, breads, and roasts come from the Lees' gardens ashore. Fresh hand-whipped cream along with a chocolate-dipped strawberry top the strawberry shortcake. Ice cream made in two six-quart freezers is hand-cranked aboard the schooner. Of course, a Maine Lobster Picnic is part of every cruise.

Guests are always welcome in the galley, whether they want to help chop vegetables, learn about making bread, or simply enjoy the camaraderie of others. Because of the size of the galley, it is a favorite gathering spot; to get out of the sun for a little

while during the day, or to listen to Doug's stories, enjoy a game of cards, or simply read by the cozy lamplight in the evening.

Leave No Trace may be a mindset that has received more attention recently, but for Doug and Linda, it has been a way of life since they started sailing their first schooner. Each time they go ashore for a Lobster Picnic, they carry out what was carried in, plus anything else that doesn't belong in the natural state of the environment. A custom-made fire pan contains the picnic fire, which is built with wood brought from the schooner. Doug and Linda even bring their own marshmallow sticks for the s'mores.

Ever since *Heritage* first set sail, the crew included the captains and their two daughters, Clara and Rachel. The girls, now adults and on their own, return as often as they can to sail with their parents. That feeling of being part of the family is important to the more than 60 percent of the *Heritage*'s guests who are repeat passengers or have been referred by someone who has sailed before. When asked how their trip was, many say, "It's the best vacation I've ever had."

ABOVE: Rachel Lee, proud baker.

BELOW LEFT: Captain Linda Lee, out for a row.

Heritage
Captains Douglas K. and Linda J. Lee
Length on deck: 95 feet
Length overall: 145
Guests: 30
(207) 594-8007
(800) 648-4544
info@schoonerheritage.com
www.schoonerheritage.com

Tomato and Herb Dip

This recipe makes good use of ripe summer tomatoes and fresh herbs.

8 ounces cream cheese, softened

2 cups chopped ripe tomatoes

½ cup chopped fresh herbs (any combination of oregano, sage, basil, and chives)

2 tablespoons dried basil

4 tablespoons Parmesan cheese

Salt and black pepper, to taste

Crackers or garlic toast, for serving

SERVES 4-6

In a bowl, mix the chopped tomatoes and their juices into the cream cheese, stirring and mashing with a wooden spoon until thoroughly combined.

Add the herbs and Parmesan cheese and stir to combine. Season to taste with salt and black pepper. Chill for 1 hour before serving. Serve with crackers or garlic toasts.

Anadama Bread

Linda Lee, co-captain of the *Heritage*, was one of the first cooks in the fleet to make all their baked goods from scratch. Molasses and cornmeal give this loaf its characteristic flavor.

Dissolve the yeast and sugar in ⅓ cup of the warm water. Set aside until foamy.

In a small bowl mix together the remaining water with the molasses, vegetable oil, salt, and cornmeal. Add this mixture to the yeast mixture.

Add the flours and mix to form a dough. Turn the dough onto a floured surface and knead for about 5 minutes until a smooth, elastic dough is formed, adding more flour as needed if the dough is too soft or sticky. Place in a greased bowl, cover, and let rise until doubled in size.

Knead the dough for 2–3 minutes, then place back in the bowl, cover, and let rise again until doubled in size.

Grease a 9×5×2½-inch loaf pan. Knead the dough again for 2–3 minutes, then shape into a loaf and place in the prepared pan. Cover and let rise until doubled in size.

Preheat the oven to 350 degrees and bake loaf 30 minutes, until golden brown and cooked through. To test, remove loaf from the pan to see that it is golden brown on the bottom. If it is still light, cook until golden brown. Let cool 10 minutes in the pan, then unmold and cool on a wire rack.

1 ⅓ cup warm water

1 tablespoon yeast

1 teaspoon sugar

⅓ cup molasses

1 tablespoon vegetable oil

1 tablespoon salt

½ cup corn meal

½ cup whole wheat flour

2 cups white flour, more if needed

MAKES 1 LOAF

Spinach Lasagna

This is a great dish for a crowd and makes use of the *Heritage* galley's homemade marinara sauce.

In a bowl, combine the ricotta, cottage cheese, eggs, Italian seasoning, nutmeg, salt, and pepper. Set aside.

Preheat the oven to 350 degrees. Grease a non-reactive 9×13-inch baking pan. Spread two cups of marinara sauce over the bottom of the pan.

Place a layer of noodles over the sauce. Add more sauce, a layer of spinach, the ricotta mixture, mozzarella. Continue to layer ending with a layer of noodles on top.

Top with the remaining marinara sauce and sprinkle the remaining mozzarella over the top. Bake at 350 for 45 minutes to 1 hour, until noodles are tender and lasagna is golden brown and bubbly.

Marinara Sauce

In a saucepan, sauté the onions and garlic in the olive oil until onions are translucent and lightly browned, about 5 minutes.

Add remaining ingredients and simmer for ½ hour. Season to taste with salt and additional black pepper.

SPINACH LASAGNA

2 cups part-skim ricotta cheese

3 cups low fat cottage cheese

2 eggs

1 teaspoon Italian seasoning

Pinch nutmeg

Salt and black pepper, to taste

4 cups marinara sauce (recipe at right)

½ pound lasagna noodles, uncooked

½ pound spinach leaves, washed, stems removed

2 cups shredded mozzarella, divided

SERVES 6-8

MARINARA SAUCE

2 tablespoons olive oil

1 cup diced onion

6 cloves garlic, minced

½ teaspoon Worcestershire sauce

½ teaspoon dried thyme

½ teaspoon dried parsley

¼ teaspoon black pepper, more as needed

1 can (4-ounce) tomato paste

1 can (28 ounce) diced tomatoes

Salt, to taste

MAKES ABOUT 4 CUPS

Lemon Poppy Seed Muffins

These are a popular early morning treat aboard the *Heritage* but they're great any time of day.

3 cups flour

4 teaspoons baking powder

1 teaspoon salt

6 tablespoons butter, softened

6 tablespoons shortening

1 cup sugar

2 eggs

²⁄₃ cup milk

¹⁄₃ cup lemon juice

¹⁄₄ cup poppy seeds

4 teaspoons grated lemon zest

Glaze (recipe below)

MAKES 12 MUFFINS

Preheat the oven to 350 degrees. Grease a 12-muffin tin. In a bowl, mix together flour, baking powder, and salt. Set aside.

In a separate bowl cream the butter and shortening with the sugar until light and fluffy.

In a small bowl, whisk the eggs with the milk and lemon juice. Add the dry ingredients and the egg mixture to the butter mixture and beat just until smooth. Stir in the poppy seeds and lemon zest.

Portion the batter into the muffin tins and bake for 25 minutes, or until golden brown and the muffins spring back when pressed lightly. Cool 10 minutes. Unmold and dip tops in glaze.

GLAZE

2 cups powdered sugar

¹⁄₄ cup lemon juice

1 teaspoon vanilla extract

MAKES ABOUT
1 ¹⁄₂ CUPS

Glaze

Mix all of the ingredients together.

Perfect Yellow Cake

This is very nice with chocolate frosting and raspberry jam filling or white frosting with apricot jam filling. For a delicious variation, substitute orange juice for wine and frost with a mixture of brown sugar, chopped nuts, and melted butter.

Preheat the oven to 350 degrees. Grease and flour two 9-inch round cake pans or one 9×13-inch baking pan. In a bowl, mix together the flour, baking powder, and salt.

In another bowl, combine the sugar, eggs, oil, white wine, and vanilla. Add the dry ingredients and beat for 1 minute. Pour into prepared pans and bake for 35–40 minutes, or until golden brown and a toothpick inserted in the center comes out clean. Cool on wire racks for 10 minutes in the pans. Unmold and cool completely before frosting with your favorite chocolate or vanilla frosting.

2 ½ cups flour

2 ¼ teaspoons baking powder

½ teaspoon salt

2 cups sugar

4 eggs

1 cup vegetable oil

1 cup white wine

1 teaspoon vanilla extract

SERVES 8–10

Isaac H. Evans

IT'S A PEACEFUL DAY with a gentle breeze, but there seems to be trouble aboard *Isaac H. Evans*. She has been boarded by pirates! Coming alongside, we realize that not one of them stands more than four feet tall. Argh, mateys! It's one of the Pirate Adventure Cruises created by Captain Brenda Thomas aboard the kid-friendly schooner. With costumes, a treasure hunt, cannon firings, pirate booty, and sea chanteys, guests of all ages can live out their swashbuckling fantasies.

The pirate cruises are only one facet of the *Evans'* varied cruise schedule. With themed trips focusing on knitting, whale watching, full-moon sailing, and mind-body-spirit wellness—to name a few—there's something for everyone. One of the *Evans'* specialty adventures is the Isle au Haut Sailing and Hiking cruise. One day during the trip, Brenda finds an anchorage near Isle au Haut where everyone can venture ashore with a brown bag lunch and plenty of water to explore one of Maine's most beautiful islands and home to the most secluded part of Acadia National Park. Eighteen miles of trails offer opportunities to experience rocky shoreline, wooded uplands, marshes, bogs, a mile-long freshwater lake, and shell heaps that tell of an American Indian presence long before Champlain's arrival in 1604. Whether guests choose to stroll the island road or trek up a park trail, they'll find the scenery stunning and peaceful.

Twenty years ago, the owner of the *Evans* began scheduling special family trips. In 1999, as the new owner, Captain Brenda decided to welcome children on all but the week-long cruises and before long kids six and older were welcome on all of the *Evans'* cruises, earning the vessel the reputation of "the family boat." Trips aboard the *Evans* include lots of time exploring ashore as well as activities and foods designed to keep the whole family happy. But not all her sailings are filled with young children. Guests come from a wide range of age groups, and multigenerational family charters have become increasingly popular.

A favorite adventure of any young *Evans* guest is searching for fairy houses on the coastal islands. These tiny dwellings in the woods or fields are built for magical inhabitants and are decorated with nature's own accessories—pinecones, driftwood, bark, wildflowers, rocks, shells, and other found objects. They can be elaborate structures with ladders and roofs, or simple abodes nestled into a hollow log.

secluded coves where the bowsprit seems to swing over the shore. Each evening Brenda will anchor the schooner in a quiet harbor where guests can stargaze far away from any city lights or go exploring in one of two rowboats brought along on every trip. From the smell of the wood stove and coffee in the morning to taking a turn at the helm and enjoying a sunset in a peaceful harbor, each day leaves guests more relaxed than the one before.

Captain Brenda was a relative newcomer to sailing when she first came aboard—in a former life, she was a banker. In a "life's-too-short" decision, she made a career change and joined the *Evans* crew as mess mate in 1995. She crewed as cook and mate during subsequent seasons and accumulated additional experience during winter-time boat deliveries to warmer climates. Within four years, she purchased the *Evans* and earned her captain's license. She traded in business suits, permed hair, makeup, and high heels for a pony tail and the many hats a captain must wear: mechanic, electrician, carpenter, plumber, painter, weatherman, navigator, teacher, and camp counselor.

As you can imagine, life as a schooner owner and captain was quite the change. Brenda is a hands-on person, each year working side-by-side with the crew on the *Evans'* repairs and maintenance. In the off-season, there is always a project in process, whether varnishing, replacing planks, or repairing the cook stove. She even answers the phone and takes reservations. Unlike banking, Brenda says, the *Evans* is "not a job, it's a lifestyle." And although it's hard work, it clearly agrees with her. Once the season starts, she has a mate, a cook, a deckhand mess mate as crew, with the galley crew helping above decks when needed.

Built in 1886 at the Vannaman Shipyard in Mauricetown, New Jersey, *Isaac H. Evans* was a hardworking vessel, dredging for oysters in the waters of Delaware Bay, which at the time was the largest fishery in the United States. In 1971, she was brought to the Percy and Small Boatyard in Bath, Maine, (now a part of the Maine Maritime Museum) to be refitted for carrying guests, and she has been lovingly maintained ever since. In honor of her historic significance, *Isaac H. Evans* was designated a National Historical Landmark in 1991. If you return to the town where she was built, as Captain Brenda has, you can visit the *Isaac H. Evans* display at the Mauricetown Historical Society and walk the shore where the *Evans* came to life. Brenda dreams of one day sailing the *Evans* to New Jersey to revisit the shipyard where she was constructed.

Isaac H. Evans' beginnings as an oyster boat mean she is a shoal-draft vessel with a centerboard. Her six-foot draft allows for exploring the nooks and crannies of the Maine coast that deeper boats can't manage. Guests often find themselves wondering how the crew succeeded in sailing into

Brenda actively embraces socially responsible business practices through community involvement, donations, volunteerism, implementation of onboard recycling and compost programs, and supporting environmental causes through Leave No Trace training and participation in coastal clean-ups. Each season starts with a special four-hour day sail (lunch included) to benefit a local charity. Whenever possible Brenda purchases produce and supplies locally, and hires local craftsmen for repair projects. Participating in community supported agriculture supplies the galley with the freshest in-season produce available and her focus on Maine-made products supports the local economy. These practices were undoubtedly the basis for Brenda and the *Evans* receiving a Maine Tourism Award in 2001.

Food is plentiful and tasty aboard the *Evans*, miraculously appearing from a galley with minimal space and from a cook stove that dates back to 1904. Three delicious meals are supplemented by an afternoon snack (essential for active pirates); snacks and fresh fruit are always on hand.

Breakfasts are hearty, and might include bacon and eggs; pancakes and sausage; or French toast along with a variety of fruit, muffins, breads, pastries, granola, and cereal. Lunches are equally sustaining with soups, chowders, stews, salads, and sandwiches, not to mention cookies, brownies, and bars for dessert. As Brenda says, "Dinner is always just too much food!" Some of the *Evans* galley specialties are beef and pork roasts, turkey with all the trimmings, and side dishes that may include seasonal vegetables from the captain's garden. Desserts (if you have room) might include crisps, cobblers, pies, hand-cranked ice cream, and other goodies—all with real,

hand-whipped cream. The galley crew is skilled at accommodating special dietary needs whether an allergy or a preference . . . important when there are young pirates aboard. Every trip includes a lobster bake on the beach of an uninhabited island. Appetites are strong after a day of sailing and the island offers everyone a chance to stretch their legs. Good summer weather encourages swimming from the beach and evening breezes invite gathering around the campfire. As on some of the other vessels, the Lobster Bake is the cook's night off, and you'll find the captain herself serving lobster, mussels, clams, hot dogs, hamburgers, corn, and side dishes—complete with champagne or sparkling cider as a perfect accompaniment. There also are vegetarian options. Watermelon and s'mores are the classic desserts. "The sky's the limit," she says. "We don't cut corners on anything—quality or quantity."

Special touches aboard the *Isaac H. Evans* reflect the captain's attention to detail. Brenda recently adorned each cabin with new quilts and pillows, as well as her hand-sewn balsam pillows, made from pieces of old sailcloth. Each cabin has a soapstone bed-warmer for chilly evenings, souvenir mugs, toiletries, and bud vases with fresh flowers.

For all these cozy amenities, Captain Brenda is a skilled and adventurous sailor. And although she's not out to force nautical education on anyone (in her words, "we're out there to have a good time"), it would be hard to spend time on the *Evans* without gaining some valuable knowledge about sailing, seamanship, and the natural world. And if you have a daughter who thinks sea captains all have gray beards and smoke pipes, Brenda ably demonstrates that there is another option.

ABOVE: **Anchored off an uninhabited island.**

BELOW: **Guests standing on the boom with the mainsail for a backrest.**

Isaac H. Evans
Captain Brenda
  and Brian Thomas
Length on deck: 65 feet
Length overall: 99 feet
Guests: 22
(877) 238-1325
www.evans@midcoast.com
www.MaineSailingAdventures.com

Zucchini Quick Bread

This recipe makes great use of the typical summer bumper crop of zucchini.

1 ½ cups flour

½ teaspoon salt

½ teaspoon baking soda

⅛ teaspoon baking powder

1 ½ teaspoons cinnamon

2 eggs

1 cup sugar

½ cup vegetable oil

1 teaspoon vanilla

1 cup grated raw zucchini

½ cup chopped nuts

MAKES 1 LOAF

Preheat oven to 350 degrees. Grease and flour a 9×5×2½-inch loaf pan. Sift together flour, salt, baking soda, baking powder, and cinnamon. Set aside.

In a bowl, whisk together eggs, sugar, vegetable oil, and vanilla. Add the flour mixture to the egg mixture along with the zucchini and chopped nuts and stir until smooth.

Pour into prepared pan and bake at 350 degrees for 1 hour, or until a toothpick inserted into the center comes out clean. Cool in the pan for 10 minutes. Run a knife around the edge of the bread and remove loaf from pan. Cool on a wire rack.

Marinated Mushrooms

This versatile side dish needs to be made a couple of days ahead in order to let the mushrooms absorb all the flavors of the onions, garlic, and herbs.

In a bowl, whisk together all of the ingredients except the mushrooms. Add the mushrooms and allow to marinate for 2 to 3 days, stirring occasionally.

½ cup extra virgin olive oil

1 cup red wine vinegar

¼ cup diced red onion

2 tablespoons sugar

1 tablespoon minced fresh garlic

½ teaspoon black pepper

Pinch red pepper flakes

1 ½ teaspoons minced fresh oregano (may substitute a pinch of dried oregano)

½ teaspoon salt

1 ½ pounds medium-sized fresh mushrooms, cleaned and trimmed.

SERVES 4-6

Isaac H. Evans Pretty Darn Good Pasta Salad

4 cups cooked rotini
(about 3 cups dried)

3 tablespoons extra virgin
olive oil

1 head roasted garlic*

½ cup sliced sun-dried
tomatoes

6 artichoke hearts,
quartered

3 or 4 hearts of palm,
sliced

¼ cup sliced pitted black
olives

1 tablespoon capers

½ cup diced green or red
peppers (or a mixture
of both)

¼ cup sliced scallions

½ cup garbanzo beans

2 tablespoons minced
fresh basil

½ cup grated Parmesan
cheese

½ cup mayonnaise

¼ cup vinaigrette dressing
(bottled or homemade)

salt and pepper, to taste

This recipe was created by the *Evans*' former cook, Eileen, who often made it for their kid's trips. Eileen called it her No"Toy"Rious Pasta Salad as she would delve into her "Toy Box" for ingredients like sun-dried tomatoes, artichoke hearts, hearts of palm or whatever struck her fancy!

Combine all ingredients in a bowl and toss well to combine. Refrigerate 1 hour before serving.

*To roast garlic: Preheat oven to 350 degrees. Lay a sheet of foil over a pie pan and drizzle the foil with 2 tablespoons of olive oil. Peel an entire head of garlic and place the peeled cloves on the foil, tossing a bit to evenly coat each clove with oil. Fold the edges of the foil to create a sort of little bowl around the garlic. Roast at 350 degrees for about 20 minutes, until garlic is golden brown and soft all the way through.

SERVES 4-6

Sweet and Sour Kielbasa

This simple, kid-friendly dish is a favorite of the young buccaneers aboard the *Isaac H. Evans*.

1 ½ pounds kielbasa

½ cup ketchup

½ cup sugar

1 cup crushed pineapple,
 with the juices

SERVES 4

Preheat the oven to 375 degrees.
Cut the kielbasa into 1-inch pieces
and arrange in an 8×8-inch casserole pan.

In a small bowl, stir together
ketchup, sugar, and pineapple.
Pour over the kielbasa and stir
to coat. Bake at 375 degrees for
30–40 minutes or until the sauce
starts to bubble and the kielbasa
browns. Serve over steamed
white rice.

Black and White Chocolate Chunk Cookies

Thanks to a letter written by a passenger aboard the *Isaac H. Evans*, Eileen's recipe appeared in the August 2006 issue of *Bon Appetit* magazine.

Preheat oven to 350 degrees. Spray 2 baking sheets with nonstick spray. In a medium bowl, whisk together flour, cocoa powder, baking soda, and salt. Set aside.

In the bowl of an electric mixer, cream together the sugars, shortening, and butter until light and fluffy. Beat in the eggs and vanilla.

Add the dry ingredients and beat just to combine. Stir in the white chocolate and pecans.

Drop by tablespoonfuls, about 2 inches apart, onto the prepared cookie sheets. Flatten slightly. Bake at 350 degrees until just set, about 12-14 minutes. Cool on racks. Store at room temperature in an airtight container.

2 cups all purpose flour

¾ cup unsweetened cocoa powder

1 teaspoon baking soda

¾ teaspoon salt

¾ cup sugar

¾ cup packed light brown sugar

½ cup vegetable shortening

½ cup butter

2 eggs

1 teaspoon vanilla

12 ounces white chocolate, coarsely chopped

1 cup coarsely chopped pecans

MAKES 5 DOZEN

Lewis R. French

WHEN WE FIRST MET Captain Garth Wells of the schooner *Lewis R. French*, he was engaged in a friendly duel of practical jokes with another schooner captain. It was his turn to retaliate, and he had a somewhat piratical glint in his eye. He wouldn't reveal exactly what he had in mind, but he clearly relished the challenge.

Captain Garth is a man who loves his work and loves his boat. Garth and his wife, Captain Jenny Tobin, describe themselves not as the owners of the *French*, but as her "caretakers." He says the *French* has "never been let go, she has always had an owner that has taken care of her, and now it is our turn to do so." Garth sailed aboard the *French* as first mate for five years before buying her in 2004. He takes great pride in his vessel, both in sailing and maintaining her, and enjoys sharing the whole experience with his guests. Plus, he's not averse to a bit of fun.

Launched in April 1871, the *French* is the oldest windjammer in the Maine fleet and almost certainly the oldest commercial schooner operating in the United States. The *French* was built in Christmas Cove, near South Bristol, Maine, not in a shipyard but in the backyard of the French brothers who named the schooner for their father. Although she seems exotic today, the *French* was the equivalent of a nineteenth-century seagoing truck: tough, reliable, fast, and ready to take on any job. Her different owners used her to carry various freights: bricks, lumber, granite, sardine cans, and even Christmas trees. She also worked a stint as a fishing boat. The *French* has been designated a National Historic Landmark.

The *French* was built specifically to sail Maine waters. Some of her cargo runs took her as far away as Boston, Massachusetts, or Nova Scotia, but her home port has always been in Maine. At sixty-five feet on deck, the *French* is a midsized coasting schooner easily sailed by a small crew and handy enough to get in and out of shallow harbors. Her size is still one of her attractions, carrying only twenty-two guests and four crew: captain, mate, cook, and cook's assistant. With such small groups, everyone quickly becomes part of the *French* "family."

After one hundred years of carrying cargo, the *French* was purchased by John Foss (who now owns the windjammer *American Eagle*) and rebuilt to carry passengers. Most likely this was the *French*'s third rebuild. It was a massive undertaking, and intensive effort was put into restoring her

TOP: Lunch is usually served on deck.

ABOVE: The *Lewis R. French* scuds along with all sails flying.

to the way she had been built originally. Oak frames were replaced, a new pine deck was laid, new spars were turned, masts were reinstalled, and the cargo hold was replaced with beautiful guest cabins and a galley. The engine—which had been installed in the 1920s—was removed and replaced by the faithful yawl boat *Greyhound*, and the *French* once again was ready to sail the Maine coast. The French brothers would have been proud.

On board the *French* today, things are kept as traditional as possible. All the sails are hoisted by hand, often with guests pitching in and learning the ropes. The anchor is raised by a traditional hand-cranked windlass. The cookstove burns wood, almost four cords per season, and heats water for showers. Instead of refrigerators, the *French* carries two iceboxes, one on deck for guests and one for the cook. Ice is brought aboard at the beginning of each trip, although these days it comes in bags and not cut from a local pond the previous winter. While the *French* does have modern electronics for communication and navigation, Garth likes to use traditional techniques as much as possible.

However, if the fog settles in, it is nice to have the radar, VHF radio, and Global Positioning System (GPS) for safety.

Nowadays, the *French* can be seen cruising as far west as Boothbay Harbor for the Windjammer Days Festival and as far east as remote Schoodic Point, that lonely promontory reaching into the Atlantic east of Bar Harbor. Every couple of years, the *French* stretches her legs and heads down to Boston for the city's Tall Ships Festival. Her season starts on Memorial Day weekend and she sails into October. The autumn sails have become very popular, combining great winds with views of the changing Maine foliage.

One of the *French*'s favorite destinations is Bucks Harbor, at the head of beautiful Eggemoggin Reach. The *French* has special ties to this pristine anchorage because it was her home port in the 1920s. Other favorite stops include Frenchboro, Long Island—a remote island village without regular ferry service and with only forty year-round residents. Garth also enjoys anchoring among the islands of Blue Hill Bay, which offer many scenic walking trails.

The day starts early for a cook on the *French*—4:30 a.m.—to get muffins (the Orange-Chocolate Muffins in this chapter's recipes are a favorite) and coffee ready for the first risers. The cook tries to get all the baking done before getting under way. Not only is it easier to cook while at anchor, but the galley crew may be needed on deck for sail and anchor handling during the day. The cooks love this dual role: it gets them up on deck with the guests, the wind, and the stunning scenery.

Soups, salads, and delicious homemade breads make up lunch, which usually is served under way. Dinner consists of large homestyle meals and plenty of food. Garth and Jenny know that the sea air stirs up serious appetites, so they provision accordingly.

Regarding desserts, Garth has some simple rules: strawberry shortcake on the first day and brownies on ice cream day. The ice cream is made aboard, and all the guests help crank the mixer. A famous dessert on board is the Maine Crazy Pudding, a legend unto itself. Sometimes it's referred to as the "dynamic dessert" as it changes shape, taste, and ingredients depending on the cook's whims, the weather, and the alignment of the stars.

Another *French* favorite is Johnny Cakes—sometimes called cornbread. If you would like to start a culinary "discussion," ask where the term Johnny Cake comes from. Garth has his ideas; the cooks have theirs. Downeast Maine, Rhode Island (which has two types of cakes: thick and thin), and the Bahamas all are debatable answers. And where does the name "Johnny" or "Jonny" come from? A local American Indian tribe? A corruption of "Journey" Cake? The *French's* recipe for Johnny Cakes appears later in this chapter.

The delicious food is just one of the reasons folks enjoy sailing on the *French*. Some come for the history, some come for the camaraderie, some come to be part of the working crew. Still others come for the simple serenity of sailing the Maine islands. The *French* has a loyal following. When we were aboard in August, quite a few of the guests were "repeats." Some had even been aboard earlier that summer. It's not uncommon for guests to feel so attached to the *French* that they take home small projects for the winter: carving a new nameboard, painting some blocks, or sewing a new ship's flag. It is clear that the *French* is well loved, and will continue to be a common and welcome sight along the Maine coast, just as she has been since 1871.

TOP: Enjoying the view from the bowsprit.

ABOVE: Rowing one of the small boats.

LEFT: A calm anchorage off Fort Point.

Lewis R. French
Captains Garth Wells
  and Jenny Tobin
Length on deck: 64 feet
Length overall: 101 feet
Guests: 22
(207) 594-2241
(800) 469-4635
captain@schoonerfrench.com
www.schoonerfrench.com

Orange-Chocolate Muffins

These colorful treats are often served with coffee first thing in the morning aboard the *French*.

2 cups flour

½ cup sugar

1 tablespoon baking powder

½ teaspoon salt

2 eggs, beaten

¼ cup orange juice

⅓ cup melted butter

2 squares (2 ounces) semi-sweet chocolate, melted*

Grated zest of 1 orange

MAKES 2 DOZEN

Preheat the oven to 400 degrees. Lightly grease 2 muffin tins (24 muffins total). In a large bowl, combine the flour, sugar, baking powder, and salt.

In a separate bowl, combine the eggs, orange juice, and melted butter. Stir the egg mixture into the dry ingredients and mix just until smooth. Divide the batter into two separate bowls.

Stir the melted chocolate into one half of the batter. Stir the grated orange zest into the other half.

Tip the muffin pans and spoon in the orange batter. Tip the pans the other way and spoon in the chocolate batter. Bake 20 minutes, or until muffins spring back when pressed lightly with the thumb.

*If desired (or if you are in a hurry), omit the melted chocolate and do not divide the batter in half. Instead, add 1½ cups mini chocolate chips to the batter along with the orange zest.

Italian Sausage Soup

This soup makes a meal in itself. You don't need to use an expensive red wine for this soup, just something you wouldn't mind drinking—especially since a glass of red wine is the perfect partner for this hearty soup! You could use turkey sausage and omit the pasta for a lighter version.

Remove and discard the casings from the sausage and break the meat into pieces. In a large stockpot, sauté the sausage in the olive oil with the garlic and onions until the sausage is browned. Pour off all excess fat and drain sausage well on paper towels. Return sausage, garlic, and onions to pot.

Add the tomatoes, beef stock, red wine, parsley, and basil. Bring to a boil, then reduce heat and simmer 45 minutes.

Add the peppers and zucchini and simmer 20 minutes.

About 15 minutes before serving, stir in the pasta and simmer until the pasta is just cooked through, about 12 minutes. Serve with fresh grated Parmesan.

2 ½ pounds sweet or hot Italian sausage, or a mixture of both

1 tablespoon olive oil

¼ cup minced garlic

2 cups chopped onion

2 cans (28-ounce) Italian-style tomatoes

4 ½ cups beef stock

½ cup dry red wine

4 tablespoons minced fresh parsley

1 tablespoon dried basil

1 cup chopped green pepper

1 cup chopped red pepper

2 cups chopped zucchini

1 pound bowtie pasta

Freshly grated Parmesan cheese, for garnish

SERVES 6-8

Simple Savory Baked Fish

This recipe couldn't be simpler, or more satisfying. The acidity of the citrus and vinegar create the perfect balance.

1 stick butter

⅓ cup cider vinegar

⅓ cup Worcestershire sauce

⅓ cup lemon juice

¼ cup Dijon mustard

4 pounds boneless haddock fillets

1 ½ cups breadcrumbs

SERVES 8

Preheat the oven to 350 degrees. Lightly grease a 9×13-inch baking pan. Melt the butter in a medium saucepan with the vinegar, Worcestershire sauce, lemon juice, and mustard.

Coat the fish fillets with the butter mixture, reserving a little of the sauce to drizzle over at the end. Dredge the fillets in breadcrumbs, place in prepared pan and bake at 350 degrees for 20–25 minutes, or until the fish is flaky and tender (cover the fish with foil if it begins to brown too much before it is cooked through). Drizzle the remaining sauce over the baked fish.

Johnny Cake

Served as a side dish for soup and stews, this traditional skillet cornbread is a favorite from the *French*'s galley.

1 cup flour

1 ½ cups cornmeal

1 teaspoon baking soda

½ teaspoon salt

2 eggs

½ cup firmly packed
   brown sugar

1 ½ cups buttermilk

1 stick butter, melted

SERVES 8-10

Preheat the oven to 400 degrees. Preheat a 10-inch cast iron skillet in the oven. In a bowl, combine the flour, cornmeal, baking soda, and salt.

In a separate bowl, whisk the eggs with the brown sugar until light and fluffy. Stir in the buttermilk and mix well.

Add the dry ingredients to the buttermilk mixture. Mix gently until just blended.

Use a small amount of the butter to grease the hot skillet. Add the remaining butter to the cornmeal batter and mix until just blended.

Pour the batter into the skillet and bake at 400 for 35 minutes or until golden brown and the cornbread springs back when lightly pressed. Cool for 10 minutes, then cut into wedges and serve warm.

Maine Crazy Pudding

According to the captain, this dish never comes out exactly the same way twice—but it's always delicious. It's a perennial favorite aboard the *French*.

For the bottom layer:

Preheat the oven to 350 degrees. Grease a 9×13-inch baking pan. In a large bowl, cream together the sugar and butter.

In another bowl, combine the flour, baking powder, baking soda, salt and nutmeg.

Add the dry ingredients to the butter mixture alternately with the milk, mixing just to combine after each addition. Fold in the raisins and spread the mixture over bottom of the prepared baking pan.

For the topping:

Combine all of the topping ingredients and pour over the bottom layer. Bake at 350 degrees for 25 minutes, or until the top is firm and lightly browned. Serve warm in bowls, topped with whipped cream.

FOR THE BOTTOM LAYER:

⅔ cup sugar

2 ½ tablespoons butter

1 ¼ cups flour

1 ¼ teaspoons baking powder

1 ¼ teaspoons baking soda

¾ teaspoon salt

¾ teaspoon nutmeg

¾ cup milk

½ cup raisins

FOR THE TOPPING:

1 ¼ cups brown sugar

2 ½ tablespoons butter

2 ½ cups boiling water

2 tablespoons plus one teaspoon lemon juice

SERVES 8-10

Mary Day

CAPTAINS BARRY KING and Jennifer Martin are, as they say, living the dream. The setting for this dream is an elegant schooner, *Mary Day*, the first of the Maine windjammer fleet to be built especially for the passenger trade. Just as Barry and Jen's beloved vessel seems ideally suited to the task, so do the couple. It's clear from spending time with the husband-and-wife team that *Mary Day* is far more than a business. As Jen says, "We came aboard the *Mary Day* together, we were married on board in 1995, and now we are raising our two children on board."

Barry and Jen are Coast Guard-licensed masters with many years of experience in seamanship and education. In fact, they first met while studying for master's degrees in experiential environmental education at the Audubon Society's Expedition Institute in 1988. Studies took Barry and Jen from a sub-Arctic village in Labrador to Death Valley in the western United States, where they researched endangered species. So you can expect to have fun aboard *Mary Day* and to learn something as well, if you are so inclined. Passengers are welcome to take part in running the ship, whether it's learning a bit about navigating coastal Maine, how to man the helm or hoist the sails, or how to use the peapod rowing boats to explore ashore. As you would expect, Barry and Jen bring a wealth of information about the environment, and love to help point out ospreys, bald eagles, porpoises, harbor seals, and the occasional whale that guests are likely to encounter. And the pair love watching their guests experience something new.

In addition to his many years with *Mary Day*, Barry has worked aboard a variety of vessels—from tugboats to square riggers—sailing from Newfoundland to the Caribbean and the Gulf of Mexico. Barry also is a registered Maine guide and a wilderness emergency medical technician (EMT). Jen's sailing experience has taken her from the Bahamas to Maine, where she was the captain of the *Figaro IV*, a classic ocean-racing yacht.

About the schooner herself? *Mary Day* is steady, stable, and comfortable, but also is built for speed, able to cruise happily at ten knots—often winning the annual schooner race each July. With a deck length of ninety feet, a beam (or width) of twenty-three feet, a layout that is clean and uncluttered, and a maximum capacity of twenty-eight passengers, there is plenty of room to stretch out with a good book,

ABOVE: Jen and Barry with their children Courtney and Sawyer.

BELOW: *Mary Day* anchored off a working waterfront.

sunbathe, or chat with friends.

Launched in 1962, *Mary Day* was the first passenger ship built in the twentieth century. Her graceful lines and seaworthy construction have earned her a first-rate reputation. Below decks, cabins are cozy, but have plenty of headroom and skylights that open for fresh air. Each cabin has a washbasin with fresh water, towels, clean, crisp sheets, comforters, and wool blankets. And, as if the usual schooner amenities weren't enough, *Mary Day* has an innovative, wood-fired heating system to ward off the chill on those occasional cool nights. There are two heads (or toilets) as well as private hot and cold freshwater showers on deck.

Life aboard, as with the other schooners in the Maine windjammer fleet, is relaxed and spontaneous. Daily destinations are determined by wind and tide, not by a rigorous itinerary. Because *Mary Day* has a centerboard (a kind of skeg that drops down from the keel), which can be raised and lowered, the vessel can make her way into secluded, smaller anchorages where boats with a deeper draft would have trouble entering.

Captain Barry, in addition to his environmental and seafaring expertise, is an accomplished folk musician, with a great voice and guitar style. He loves to entertain his guests, who are encouraged to bring along their instruments. In the main saloon, there is a fireplace for cool evenings as well as a parlor organ for those with keyboard talents. In fact, the *Mary Day*'s summer itinerary usually includes the Sweet Chariot Folk Festival held annually on Swan's Island in East Penobscot Bay. Barry and Jen also feature lighthouse cruises, natural history cruises, and photography cruises. There also is a hands-on, physically active, sail-training adventure that is held in connection with the WoodenBoat School. As Barry says, "We've created a tradition of teaching and learning aboard that we and our guests value." The number of repeat customers attests to this.

Daily trips ashore are for wandering, hiking, exploring, swimming, and, of course, the Lobster Picnic, without which no windjammer voyage would be complete. But all-you-can-eat lobster is just one of the culinary attractions aboard. Ship's cook Mary Barney, author of the cookbook *Ring That Bell*, has been with Barry and Jen since 1998 and previously worked for twenty-five summers on Monhegan Island as a baker, a skill that serves her well on *Mary Day*. Breads, pies, rolls, cookies, and sticky buns are handmade and baked in an antique, wood-burning stove. In fact, Mary's Sour Cream Apple Pie won the Windjammer Weekend Schooner Pie Baking Contest in 2004. (We've included her recipe in this chapter.) The galley is open, and guests are free to poke their heads in to say hello or to get a whiff of the tantalizing aromas that signal—along with the ringing of the ship's bell—when the meal will be served. Breakfast and supper are served family style in the spacious main cabin. Lunch can be enjoyed on deck.

"We serve traditional New England fare—hearty and homemade, with generous portions. We use local ingredients," Jen says. "Our passengers tell us that our food reminds them of things their grandma used to make—things like chowders, fresh breads, and a traditional Thanksgiving turkey dinner with all the trimmings."

Hearty and traditional, yes, but with some great updated standards such as the Seafood Smorgasbord with Parmesan Baked Scallops, Garlicky Shrimp, and Creamed Crabmeat served on pasta with herbs and sun-dried tomatoes. This might

be accompanied by Lemony Caesar Salad and bread fresh out of the oven. As Mary says, "It's good, homemade food—except you don't have to make it yourself!"

Not only do Barry and Jen sail as a family, they consider their guests as a part of their family. Through the years, the couple has come to know their guests' extended families, and pictures from home often are shared. This type of easy companionship aboard has led to more than a few lasting friendships. "Sailing *Mary Day* here on the Maine coast is a dream made complete because of the amazing people who share the excitement and wonder of each week's experience. Every week, we get a chance to see the coast through new eyes, so we are always learning, always sharing." Can anything be better than a week filled with great sailing, great scenery, great food, and great companionship?

TOP: *Mary Day*'s impressive cloud of sails.

ABOVE: The comfortable saloon.
LEFT: Traditional food, updated and beautifully presented.

Mary Day
Captains Barry King
 and Jennifer Martin
Length on deck: 90 feet
Length overall: 125 feet
Guests: 28
(800) 992-2218
captains@schoonermaryday.com
www.schoonermaryday.com

Sticky Buns

This signature breakfast treat is a passenger favorite—for obvious reasons!

FOR THE DOUGH:

½ cup warm water

1 tablespoon yeast

⅓ cup sugar

⅓ cup butter

½ cup milk

1 egg

1 teaspoon salt

3 ½ cups flour, more as needed

1 teaspoon cardamom

FOR THE STICKY MIXTURE:

¾ cup butter

⅔ cup brown sugar

2 tablespoons molasses

FOR THE FILLING:

¼ cup sugar

1 teaspoon cinnamon

2 tablespoons butter, melted

½ cup raisins

½ cup chopped walnuts, optional

SERVES 4-6

Make the dough:

Sift together the 3½ cups flour, salt, and the cardamom, and set aside. In a separate bowl, dissolve the yeast and 1 teaspoon of the sugar in the warm water and let sit 10 minutes until frothy.

Heat the milk in a small sauce pan with the remaining sugar and ⅓ cup of the butter. As soon as the butter is melted, remove from the heat and whisk in the egg. Cool to room temperature.

Add the milk mixture to the yeast mixture. Add the flour mixture and mix to form a dough. Turn onto a lightly floured surface and knead for 2–3 minutes, or until a soft dough is formed, adding more flour as needed if the dough is too sticky.

Place in a greased bowl, cover with plastic wrap, and let sit for about an hour, or until doubled in size (alternatively, the dough can be kept overnight in the refrigerator).

Prepare the sticky mixture:

Melt the butter in the bottom of a 9×13-inch baking pan. Sprinkle the brown sugar over the butter, then drizzle the molasses over the brown sugar. Place the pan on top of the stove over low heat and heat, without bubbling, for about a minute, until the brown sugar dissolves into the butter. Remove from the heat.

Form the sticky buns:

Whisk together the cinnamon and sugar for the filling. Have ready the melted butter, raisins, and walnuts. Turn the dough out onto a lightly floured surface and roll into an 8×15-inch rectangle. Brush the dough with the 2 tablespoons of melted butter, leaving about an inch at the top unbuttered. Sprinkle the cinnamon sugar evenly over the dough. Sprinkle the raisins and the nuts evenly over the dough. Starting with the buttered edge, roll into a log lengthwise, then slice into

Cooked-Oatmeal Bread

This is a tasty twist on standard oatmeal bread.

Dissolve the yeast and sugar in the warm water. Let stand 10 minutes until frothy.

In a separate bowl, stir together the oatmeal, milk, salt, and brown sugar. Add this mixture to the yeast mixture.

Add the flour and mix until a dough is formed. Turn onto a floured surface and knead until smooth, about 5 minutes, adding more flour as needed if dough is too sticky. Place the dough in a greased bowl, cover with a damp towel, and let rise until doubled in volume.

Grease a 9×5×2½-inch loaf pan. Punch the dough down, knead briefly, and shape into a loaf. Place in the prepared pan, cover with a damp towel, and let rise until doubled in volume.

Preheat the oven to 375 degrees. Bake the loaf for 45–50 minutes, until golden brown. For a crisper, golden crust, remove the loaf from the pans and bake for a few more minutes.

¼ cup warm water

2 ½ teaspoons dry yeast

1 teaspoon sugar

¾ cup cooked oatmeal, warm

½ cup milk, warm

1 teaspoon salt

2 tablespoons dark brown sugar

2 ½ cups flour, more as needed

MAKES 1 LOAF

Sticky Buns continued

1-inch slices. Arrange the slices, cut side down, over the sticky bun mixture in the baking pan. Flatten buns slightly, cover loosely with a clean towel, and let rise until almost doubled in size.

Preheat the oven to 375 degrees and bake the sticky buns for 25-30 minutes, until the sticky bun mixture is bubbling and the buns are golden brown. Invert immediately onto a serving platter and serve warm.

Seafood Smorgasbord
(Parmesan Baked Scallops, Garlicky Shrimp, and Creamed Crabmeat)

FOR THE BAKED SCALLOPS:

1 ¼ pounds large sea scallops

⅓ cup mayonnaise

¼ cup grated Parmesan cheese

½ cup seasoned bread crumbs

FOR THE GARLICKY SHRIMP:

2 tablespoons butter

1 teaspoon minced garlic

1 pound shrimp, peeled and deveined

Salt and pepper to taste

FOR THE CREAMED CRABMEAT:

½ pound crabmeat

1 cup heavy cream

Salt and pepper, to taste

FOR THE SHELLS:

1 pound pasta shells, cooked and
    drained

1 cup heavy cream

¾ cup Parmesan cheese

2 tablespoons minced fresh basil

2 tablespoons minced fresh parsley

½ cup sun-dried tomatoes

SERVES 4-6

Each of these seafood recipes can make a great stand-alone dish. All together, you've got a sumptuous feast!

For the baked scallops:
Preheat the oven to 375 degrees. Grease a small casserole pan. Arrange the scallops over the bottom of the pan. Mix together the mayonnaise and the Parmesan cheese and dollop a little over each scallop. Sprinkle the bread crumbs over the top and bake at 375 degrees for 15–20 minutes, until scallops are just cooked through.

For the garlicky shrimp:
Heat the butter and garlic in a skillet over medium-high heat until the butter begins to bubble. Add the shrimp and sauté until the shrimp are just cooked through. Season to taste with salt and pepper.

For the creamed crabmeat:
In a saucepan over medium heat, gently heat the crabmeat with the cream until it just begins to bubble. Season to taste with salt and pepper.

For the shells:
In a pot, combine the shells with the remaining ingredients and cook over medium heat until heated through and evenly combined.

To serve:
Divide each of the seafood dishes evenly between 4 to 6 dinner plates. Serve with a spoonful of the shells.

Mary Day Caesar Salad

Guests particularly enjoy this tangy version of the classic Caesar.

Cut or tear the Romaine lettuce into bite-sized pieces and place in a large bowl. Pour the dressing over the top and sprinkle salad with the croutons, cashews, Baby Swiss cheese, and Parmesan cheese evenly over the dressing. Toss well to combine. Serve immediately.

4 Romaine lettuce hearts

1 cup Lemony Caesar dressing (recipe below)

2 cups croutons

½ cup freshly grated Parmesan cheese

1 cup chopped unsalted cashews

cubed Baby Swiss Cheese

SERVES 6-8

Lemony Caesar Dressing

You can make this ahead of time and let the flavors blend. Use a top quality olive oil for the best results.

In a medium-sized bowl, combine the lemon juice, lemon zest, garlic, and vinegar.

Slowly drizzle in the olive oil, whisking constantly, until smooth. Whisk in the salt and pepper.

LEMONY CAESAR DRESSING

3 tablespoons fresh lemon juice

1 teaspoon grated lemon zest

2 cloves garlic, minced

1 teaspoon white wine vinegar

⅔ cup extra virgin olive oil

1 teaspoon black pepper

½ teaspoon salt

MAKES ABOUT 1 CUP

Gussie Hodgkins, ship's cat

Sour Cream Apple Pie

Sour cream and spices provide a rich variation on the classic. Granny Smiths or other tart apples are perfect for this recipe.

Preheat the oven to 400 degrees. Arrange the apples over the bottom of the prepared pie crust.

In a bowl, beat together the egg, sour cream, vanilla, and nutmeg. Stir in the flour, sugar, and salt and pour over the apples. Bake for 15–20 minutes at 400 until the crust just starts to brown.

Reduce heat to 350 degrees, sprinkle the crumb topping evenly over the top and bake until puffy and golden, about 15 minutes.

For the crumb topping:
Mix together the sugar, flour, and cinnamon.

Cut in the butter until the mixture resembles coarse meal.

2 cups sliced apples

8 or 9-inch pie crust

1 egg

1 cup sour cream

1 teaspoon vanilla extract

¼ teaspoon nutmeg

2 tablespoons flour

¾ cup sugar

⅛ teaspoon salt

Crumb topping
(recipe below)

SERVES 8-10

CRUMB TOPPING

⅓ cup sugar

⅓ cup flour

1 teaspoon cinnamon

3 tablespoons butter,
cut into pieces

MAKES ALMOST 1 CUP

Mercantile

MERCANTILE IS ONE OF Captain Ray Williamson's three "green schooners"—so called because they are the only boats in the Maine windjammer fleet with dark green hulls. His other two, *Mistress* and *Grace Bailey*, together with the *Mercantile* make up the fleet-within-the-fleet that Ray and his wife, Ann, own.

Both *Mercantile* and *Grace Bailey* have a rich history, but *Mercantile* is a native Maine boat, built on Little Deer Isle by the Billings family and launched in 1916. *Mercantile* was built during the course of three winters by Pearl Billings; his father, John Jackson Billings; and two Billings brothers, Arthur and Walter, who designed the vessel. She is one of five schooners the family built between 1909 and 1926. The Billings Boat Yard still exists nearby on Deer Isle in Stonington, Maine.

Captain Pearl is said to have named *Mercantile* after admiring the sign in a local bank window. Since he considered it unlucky to have an odd number of letters in a ship's name, "Mercantile" fit the bill. *Mercantile* is a shoal draft schooner, meaning that the keel is shallow, allowing the vessel to pick up and discharge cargo at ports in shallower waters that larger, deeper vessels can't access. Before trucking

took over most of the cargo-hauling duties in the 1940s, the harbors of the eastern seaboard were full of these graceful work-horses.

For most of the year, *Mercantile* carried barrel staves and firewood, but in the fall, at the end of the fishing season, she served the Maine fishery by carrying salted hake (a member of the cod family), as so many vessels in New England's history have. From various Down East points, *Mercantile* carried the salted, dried fish to the Gorton-Pew Company in Gloucester, Massachusetts—now Gorton's of Gloucester, which still ships frozen fish across the country. After delivering the salt fish, *Mercantile* would return with a cargo of salt, ready for the next fishing season. Other occasional cargoes included coal, lumber, boxwood, and brick. Amazingly, she often was sailed by only two people, the captain and a mate, who handled everything from repairs to navigation to cooking.

Most of *Mercantile*'s cargo-carrying runs were in Maine coastal waters, but she spent two years in the coasting trade out of Providence, Rhode Island, under the watchful eye of her designer Arthur Billings. But by the 1940s, she was nearing the end of her working life, as so much

cargo hauling was being done by truck. She remained in the Billings family from her launch in 1916 right up until 1942 when she made a career change to the role she's been working in ever since.

Mercantile was purchased by Captain Frank Swift as part of his recreational cruising fleet that operated out of the lovely village of Camden, Maine. There the *Mercantile* was joined by the *Enterprise* (note the ten letters!), which also became a fleet member of Captain Swift's Maine Windjammer Cruises™.

Enter Ray and Ann Williamson. The couple, who met in college, was living in St. Croix where Ann taught kindergarten. Ray got his start as a professional sailor in the local charter-boat fleet. But perhaps it was Ray's seafaring ancestry (which he has traced to both shipbuilders and sea captains in England and Scotland) that drew him to larger, more traditional vessels. When he and Ann arrived in Camden in 1982, they knew they had found their new home. Ray signed on as a deckhand on *Grace Bailey*,

and Ann quickly found a teaching job. Ray earned his captain's license and skippered the *Mistress*. Four years later, they purchased the three green schooners of Maine Windjammer Cruises™.

When Ray and Ann purchased the three schooners, the couple recognized that all three vessels would need a major overhaul in order to be safe and comfortable. It was a massive undertaking, but Ray and Ann managed to restore all three completely. It was hard work and long hours (by now, they had two young daughters), but it also was a dream come true as Ray combined his two favorite occupations: shipbuilding and sailing.

After such a long and hard-working career, *Mercantile* certainly was entitled to some TLC and celebrated her new lease on life in 1989. During her restoration, Ray and his crew removed some of the more modern features that had been added in order to return Mercantile to a more authentic state. Water is gravity fed, flowing below from barrels on deck. *Mercantile* uses manila lines instead of synthetic, and her sails still are good, old-fashioned canvas.

To honor her history, Ray and Ann invited members of the Billings family—including Robert Billings of Stonington, who had worked aboard the schooner as mate and eventually as captain—for a heritage cruise to *Mercantile*'s former home port in Eggemoggin Reach off Little Deer Isle. As the *Mercantile* headed up the reach, a group of friends, family, and supporters unfurled a large banner from the Deer Isle Sedgwick Bridge that read: "Welcome Captain Bob and the Billings crew. She's still beautiful."

Like many of his fellow windjammer captains, Ray considers himself not only a mariner, but a preservationist and curator of what he calls their "working museum."

Mercantile is 115 feet long overall and 80 feet on deck. There are accommodations for twenty-nine passengers with fourteen double cabins (some with double berths and others with twin) and one private single cabin. There are three heads for

passengers and a freshwater shower below decks. Auxiliary power is provided by a traditional yawl boat.

Ray and Ann describe the food aboard *Mercantile* as "hearty Down East homestyle fare." All meals are cooked below decks on a wood-burning stove, which is lit at 4:30 every morning so the ship's cook can prepare baked goodies for the early risers. The delicious freshly baked muffins, blueberry buckle, or sour cream coffee cake, Ann says, "will hold you over 'til breakfast." Later, a hearty full breakfast is served.

Lunch usually is served on deck, and might include chowder, chili, lasagna, or stew, along with salads and freshly baked breads, followed by fruit and dessert. Dinners—such as Baked Stuffed Haddock and New England Boiled Dinner—are usually served at the huge, varnished galley tables below; always with lots of fresh vegetables, salads, homemade breads, and dessert.

One of Ray's specialties is the Captain's Barbeque, a festive cookout that usually is served on the last evening of the cruise. Using their special Souvlaki Marinade (see page 56 for the recipe), Ray can be found grilling ribs, chicken, and steaks that are served with an assortment of vegetarian dishes. For dessert, you might be treated to some old-fashioned, hand-churned ice cream. Ray says, "I really like standing at the grill, basting the meat, tending the flames, and spending time with passengers on deck."

On *Mercantile*'s shorter weekend and three-day cruises, the traditional Lobster Bake is combined with the Captain's Barbeque for a Surf and Turf night; freshly steamed lobsters and cooked-to-order steaks combine the best of both worlds.

TOP: Relaxing in the rigging.

ABOVE: At the helm on a calm day.

BELOW LEFT: Everyone pitches in to furl the foresail.

Mercantile

Captain Ray and Ann Williamson

Length on deck: 80 feet

Length overall: 115 feet

Guests: 29

(207) 236-2938

(800) 736-7981

sail@mainewindjammercruises.com

www.mainewindjammercruises.com

Lobster Dip

Any lobster left over from the Lobster Bake goes into this luxurious spread. It's perfect for the pre-dinner cocktail hour.

Combine all ingredients in a saucepan and cook over low heat, stirring constantly until warmed through. Serve immediately with warm garlic toasts or with crackers.

1 cup diced lobster meat

8 ounces cream cheese, softened

¼ cup shredded cheese, any variety

½ cup mayonnaise

1 teaspoon mustard powder

1 tablespoon confectioner's sugar

1 tablespoon minced onion

1 teaspoon garlic powder

¼ teaspoon salt, or to taste

Garlic toasts or crackers, for serving

SERVES 6

Garlic Toasts

These simple toasts make a perfect, savory base for lobster or other dips and spreads.

Preheat the oven to 400 degrees. Mix together the olive oil and garlic. Slice the baguette into slices about ¼ inch thick. Brush each slice lightly on both sides with the olive oil and place on a baking sheet. Sprinkle the tops lightly with salt and black pepper. Toast at 400 degrees for about 5 minutes, until very lightly browned. Serve warm.

GARLIC TOASTS

½ cup olive oil

1 tablespoon minced garlic

1 baguette

Salt and black pepper, to taste

SERVES 6

Wheat Bread

This classic hearty loaf is a staple aboard the *Mercantile*, and fills the galley with the smell of fresh-baked bread.

1 cup warm water

1 tablespoon yeast

¼ cup sugar

¼ cup oil

1 teaspoon salt

1 cup whole wheat flour,
 more as needed

1 ½ cups white flour,
 more as needed

MAKES 1 LOAF

Dissolve the yeast in the warm water. Mix in the sugar. Let stand about 20 minutes.

Add the oil, salt, and flours and mix until a dough is formed. Turn out onto a lightly floured surface and knead for 2-3 minutes, adding more flour as needed if dough is too sticky. Place in a lightly greased bowl, cover with plastic wrap and let rise until doubled in size.

When dough has doubled in size, generously grease a 9×5×2½-inch loaf pan. Punch down the dough and knead on a floured surface for about 5 minutes, until smooth. Shape into a loaf and place in the prepared pan. Let rise until almost doubled in size.

Preheat oven to 350 degrees. Bake for 35–45 minutes or until golden brown and cooked through. The bread should spring back when pressed lightly. Cool for 10 minutes in the pan, then run a knife around the edge of the pan and remove the loaf to a rack to cool completely.

New England Boiled Dinner

Guests aboard the *Mercantile* look forward to this classic New England dish. Any leftover corned beef makes great breakfast hash.

Place the brisket in a large pot with the onion, garlic, and pepper. Cover with water and bring to a boil. Reduce heat and simmer at least 2–3 hours, or until fork tender.

20 minutes before serving, add the carrots, potatoes, and cabbage and simmer until all of the vegetables are tender.

Remove the brisket and vegetables from the water and allow to drain. Slice the brisket and arrange on a serving platter with the boiled vegetables. Serve with spicy mustard or horseradish sauce.

One 5 pound corned beef brisket

1 large onion, diced

4 cloves garlic, minced

¼ teaspoon black pepper

6 carrots, peeled and sliced thick

6 potatoes, peeled and cut into quarters

1 head cabbage, quartered

SERVES 4-6

Roasted Pepper Salad

Roasting the peppers brings out their natural sweetness and combines nicely with fresh seasonal salad greens.

2 red peppers

¼ cup red wine vinegar

1 tablespoon vegetable oil

1 tablespoon water

1 tablespoon honey

1 teaspoon dried thyme

1 clove garlic, minced

Salt, to taste

½ head iceberg lettuce, washed and torn into bite-sized pieces

4 cups mixed salad greens, washed

1 cup sliced zucchini

½ cup cubed cheese, such as cheddar or mozzarella

SERVES 4

Whisk together vinegar, oil, water, honey, thyme, garlic, and salt. Set aside in the refrigerator.

Preheat oven to 450 degrees. Place whole red peppers on a pie pan and bake at 450 until the skins turn black. Remove peppers from the oven and place in a bowl. Cover the bowl tightly with plastic wrap and let sit until cool. When the peppers are cool, remove the skins, which should slip off easily, and discard. Remove the seeds and discard. Slice the peppers into thin strips.

In a large bowl combine the lettuces, zucchini, cheese, peppers, and vinegar mixture. Toss to combine. Serve immediately.

Hundred Dollar Cake

This easy-to-make cake is often served aboard to celebrate a special occasion such as a passenger's birthday. Combined with hand-churned ice cream, this is a perennial favorite.

Preheat the oven to 350 degrees. Grease a 9×13-inch baking pan. In a large bowl, sift together the flour, sugar, cocoa powder, and baking soda. Set aside.

In another bowl, whisk together the water, mayonnaise, and vanilla. Add the mayonnaise mixture to the flour mixture and beat well.

Pour batter into prepared pan and bake for 30–40 minutes, or until a toothpick inserted in the center comes out clean. Cool on rack. When cool, frost with Vanilla Buttercream Frosting.

Vanilla Buttercream Frosting

Classic buttercream frosting is the finishing touch on the delicious Hundred Dollar Cake.

Cream all of the ingredients together until smooth.

2 cups flour

1 cup sugar

¼ cup cocoa powder

2 teaspoons baking soda

1 cup cold water

1 cup mayonnaise

1 teaspoon vanilla extract

2 cups Vanilla Buttercream Frosting (recipe below)

SERVES 8-12

VANILLA BUTTERCREAM FROSTING

1 cup butter, softened

3 cups confectioner's sugar

6 tablespoons cream

1 teaspoon vanilla extract

MAKES ABOUT 2 CUPS

Mistress

WHEN RAY AND ANN WILLIAMSON decided they wanted to operate their own passenger schooner, they didn't anticipate having three. Indeed, owning one windjammer is a handful, considering an historic wooden vessel's need for meticulous care and maintenance. But when the opportunity came to buy Maine Windjammer Cruises from the previous owners, Ray and Ann decided it was all or nothing, and invested their time, money, and TLC on the three green schooners.

Mistress is unique in the windjammer fleet. With only forty-six feet on deck, she is less than half the size of the other green schooners and carries only six passengers (rather than the usual twenty or more). The experience aboard *Mistress* has some of the benefits of chartering a yacht while still providing the feel of a coasting schooner.

Built on nearby Deer Isle to be a private yacht, *Mistress*'s construction was a leisurely process. Friends and passersby often asked the owner, "You ever going to launch that boat?" But when she was finished in 1960, she was not a private yacht but went directly into the windjamming trade, where she has been the "princess" of the fleet ever since.

The *Mistress* is rigged like a traditional windjammer. She is a gaff-rigged schooner with lanyard and deadeyes. When the wind fails, she has a sixty-horsepower inboard diesel engine for propulsion; this sets her apart from most of the larger schooners, which are powered by yawl boats.

Being smaller in size has some advantages for the guests, who feel a close connection with the sailing of the schooner and an intimate connection with the maritime world around it. The crew and guests are closer to the water and the sea life, and while the *Mistress* is a solid, stable schooner, her size makes her a lively sailor.

With two in crew—the captain and the cook-mate—*Mistress* can host six guests. Sometimes the guests are from different groups, but *Mistress* is ideal for families or groups of friends.

Down below, *Mistress* has modern accommodations with three double cabins, each with its own head, sink, and access from the deck—providing a bit more privacy than on the larger windjammers. The galley/main saloon is for meals as well as lounging, reading, playing cards, or goofing off. The galley has an efficient three-burner propane stove with an oven, and the meals that come out of it are in the windjammer

TOP: In the galley

ABOVE: A gorgeous sunset on the bay.

RIGHT: Known as the "princess" of the fleet, *Mistress* is a real little ship.

tradition of great food and lots of it. With her soups, stews, breads, and cookies, *Mistress*'s galley does not take a back seat to her larger sisters. *Mistress*'s galley produces some of Ray and Ann's trademark meals, such as the Captain's Barbeque with the Williamsons' signature Souvlaki Marinade, and the Surf and Turf feast with Maine lobster and cooked-to-order steaks. As with *Mercantile* and *Grace Bailey*, Ann supervises the provisioning and the menu aboard *Mistress*, using the tried-and-true recipes that she and Ray have collected over the years.

Mistress was Captain Ray's first command in 1983, and quite a few other windjammer captains have begun their careers on the lovely little schooner. Following in her father's footsteps, Ray and Ann's daughter, Allysa earned her captain's license in 2001 and skippered the *Mistress* for two seasons. Along with her sister, Kristi, Allysa has spent summers aboard the schooners since she was six years old. Allysa presently teaches music at a school just north of Camden, Maine, and still takes the helm as relief captain during the summer.

WINDJAMMER RELIEF EFFORT

CAPTAIN RAY WILLIAMSON—who owns *Mistress, Grace Bailey,* and *Mercantile*—was vacationing with his family in Indonesia when the devastating tsunami struck in 2004. The family did what they could to help at the time, but Captain Ray soon realized that one of the biggest challenges was getting supplies to the remote islands that could be served only by ship.

Ray knew of an Indonesian ship, the two-hundred-foot motorized sailing ship KLM *Maruta Jaya,* that would be perfect for delivering much-needed supplies. In May 2005, the **Windjammer Relief Effort** chartered *Maruta Jaya* and, with a full cargo of relief supplies, headed for the Ache Province and the remote villages of Nias and the Simeulue Islands. The cargo included 652 tarpaulins; 8,280 plastic jerry cans; 77,520 water purification kits; 940 kitchen sets; 3,936 butterfly stoves; and 9,714 family kits, each containing kitchen supplies, soap, five pairs of sandals, five sarongs, and five sleeping mats.

In November 2005 and again in March 2006, after the windjammers were laid up for the winter, Captain Ray returned to Simeulue. Very little had changed in these remote districts that were without road access. The Loch Dalam village school that had been leveled by the tsunami had not been

rebuilt, but the leaky, temporary structure built with supplies from the Windjammer Relief Effort ten months earlier was still standing. The Tupperware containers delivered by *Maruta Jaya* were in use at the farewell dinner where Captain Ray promised to do whatever he could to restore the Loch Dalam school.

For more information about the Windjammer Relief Effort, visit www.windjammerreliefeffort.org.

Mistress's size brings her guests into a close relationship with wind and water.

Mistress

Captain Ray and Ann Williamson
Length on deck: 46 feet
Length overall: 60 feet
Guests: 6
(207) 236-2938
(800) 736-7981
sail@mainewindjammercruises.com
www.mainewindjammercruises.com

Pumpkin Quick Bread

1 ¾ cups flour

1 teaspoon baking soda

½ teaspoon salt

½ teaspoon cinnamon

½ teaspoon nutmeg

2 eggs

1 ½ cups sugar

½ cup oil

⅓ cup cold water

1 cup canned pumpkin

MAKES ONE LOAF

This is a perfect companion to a steaming cup of coffee. Serve with butter or cream cheese if you like.

Preheat the oven to 350 degrees. Grease and flour a 9×5×2½-inch loaf pan. In a bowl, sift together the flour, baking soda, salt, cinnamon, and nutmeg. Set aside.

In another bowl, whisk together the eggs, sugar, oil, water, and pumpkin. Combine the flour mixture with the egg mixture and mix until smooth.

Pour into the prepared pan and bake for 1 hour, or until a toothpick inserted in the center comes out clean. Cool in the pan for 10 minutes, then run a knife around the edge of the pan and remove the loaf to a rack to cool.

Cheese Strata

This savory, layered breakfast dish
is a favorite aboard the *Mistress*.

Preheat oven to 325 degrees.
Grease an 8 x 8-inch baking pan.
Arrange cubed bread in the bottom of the pan and sprinkle the
cheese over the bread.

In a bowl, whisk together the
eggs, milk, onion, mustard, salt,
and black pepper. Pour over the
bread. Sprinkle the ham or bacon
over the top.

Bake at 325 degrees for 1 hour
until golden brown and cooked
through. If the strata begins to
brown before it is done, cover
loosely with foil. Let set 10 or 15
minutes before cutting into
squares and serving.

2 cups cubed bread

1 cup shredded cheddar
    cheese

5 eggs

2 cups milk

¼ cup diced onion

½ teaspoon dry mustard

½ teaspoon salt, or to
    taste

⅛ teaspoon black pepper,
    or to taste

1 ½ cups diced ham or
    crumbled bacon

SERVES 8-10

Beef Stew

There's something about the sea air that really gives passengers an appetite. This hearty stew is the perfect way to satisfy that hunger. Serve with crusty bread on the side.

3 tablespoons vegetable oil

2 pounds beef stew meat

1 cup diced green pepper

2 cups diced onion

3 tablespoons flour

¼ teaspoon beef bouillon paste

2 cups sliced carrots

4 cups cubed peeled potatoes*

1 ½ cups chopped green beans

SERVES 4

In a large pot, heat the oil until quite hot. Add the beef, green pepper, and onion, and sauté until browned. Lower the heat, stir in the flour, and cook 2–3 minutes. Stir in the bouillon paste. Add cold water to cover and bring to a boil, stirring constantly. Reduce to a simmer and cook for 2½ hours, stirring occasionally.

Add the carrots and potatoes and cook for ½ hour, or until carrots and potatoes are completely tender.

Add the green beans and cook for 15 minutes.

*If desired, omit the potatoes and serve the stew over mashed potatoes.

Tossed Cashew Salad

1 head Green Leaf lettuce, washed and torn into bite-sized pieces

8 ounces baby spinach

2 green apples, cored and sliced thin

1 cup shredded cheddar cheese

1 cup cashew halves or pieces

Poppy seed dressing, to serve on the side

SERVES 4

POPPY SEED VINAIGRETTE

¾ cup sugar

1 teaspoon mustard powder

1 teaspoon salt

½ cup cider vinegar

1 teaspoon grated red onion

⅓ cup water

½ cup olive oil

1 ½ teaspoons poppy seeds

MAKES ABOUT 2 CUPS

This is another creation of Captain Ray's wife, Ann. Fresh apples and cashews give this salad a satisfying crunch.

In a large bowl, toss together the lettuce, spinach, apples, cheese, and cashews. Serve with poppy seed vinaigrette on the side.

Poppy Seed Vinaigrette

In a small pan whisk together the sugar, mustard, salt, vinegar, red onion, and water. Heat over medium heat until the sugar is dissolved. Do not boil.

Whisk in water, oil, and poppy seeds. Refrigerate until ready to use. Stir or shake well before serving.

Iced Gingerbread Bars

These are a favorite dessert aboard the *Mistress*, and the icing adds a festive touch.

Preheat the oven to 375 degrees. Grease a 9×13-inch baking pan. In a bowl, sift together the flour, ginger, cinnamon, allspice, salt, and baking soda. Set aside. In another bowl, beat together the sugar and butter until light and fluffy.

In another bowl, whisk together the buttermilk, molasses, and egg. Add the flour mixture and the egg mixture to the butter mixture. Pour into the prepared pan.

Bake at 375 degrees for 15–20 minutes, or until a toothpick inserted in the center comes out clean. Cool on a wire rack. When cool, drizzle the icing evenly over the top and let set about ½ hour before cutting into bars.

NOTE: Buttermilk can be replaced with a mixture of ½ cup milk mixed with 1½ teaspoons vinegar or lemon juice.

Icing
Mix all of the ingredients together.

½ cup sugar

¼ cup butter, softened

1 cup flour

1 teaspoon ground ginger

1 teaspoon cinnamon

½ teaspoon allspice

⅛ teaspoon salt

½ teaspoon baking soda

½ cup buttermilk*

¼ cup molasses

1 egg, slightly beaten

Icing (recipe below)

MAKES 8-12 BARS

ICING

1 cup powdered sugar

2 tablespoons lemon juice

1 tablespoon cream

1 ½ teaspoons vanilla extract

MAKES ABOUT ¾ CUP

Nathaniel Bowditch

THE SCHOONER *NATHANIEL BOWDITCH* has a colorful and distinguished history. It started in 1922 when she slid down the ways of the Hodgdon Brothers Shipyard in East Boothbay, Maine and got her first taste of salt water. Her graceful lines came off the drafting table of William Hand, one of the best-known yacht designers of his time. Homer Loring, a Boston lawyer commissioned the famed marine architect to design a schooner to be fast and able . . . and he got it.

Launched as *Ladona*, named for the boat Homer's father commanded in WWI, she started off as a bald headed, two-masted, gaff-rigged schooner. A few years later in 1928, she would change to a staysail schooner with a large Marconi-rigged main, which was easier to handle. In the year after launching she was entered in the famous Newport to Bermuda Race and came in fourth.

During World War II, the *Bowditch* was commissioned by the Coast Guard to search for German subs off New York Harbor. Not only did she bravely join the fray, she was twice cited by the Coast Guard's Commander of the Eastern Sea Frontier for seaworthiness in poor conditions. She proved to be safe and stalwart as well as speedy. With her deep keel (draft 10½ feet), the *Bowditch* was stable and roomy below decks, an added advantage for her current occupation.

After the war, the lively schooner became a working vessel as part of the fishing fleet in Stonington, Connecticut, where she was rigged as a dragger. In 1971 the *Bowditch* was saved from the scrap yard by American Practical Navigators Inc., and rebuilt for the passenger trade. Fittingly, the company renamed her *Nathaniel Bowditch*, after the brilliant mathematician and author of the *American Practical Navigator*, a volume that was to be the gold standard in navigation for the next 150 years.

The *Bowditch*'s speed and stability is still a source of pride for current owners Captain Owen and Cathie Dorr. They participate in the Great Schooner Race annually. On any day during a trip, the captain may spot another schooner and order, "More Sail!" Then the chase is on. If the *Bowditch* passes its competitor, the captain orders a salute with the signal cannon. With a top speed of more than ten knots, she slips through the water at an impressive clip. "She likes the open water," Owen says. Her win in the 2007 Great Schooner

The *Nathaniel Bowditch* slides by a rocky islet.

Race, Windward Class is a testament to her speed. She is presently rigged as a topsail schooner. She carries a main, fore, staysail, jib, topsail, and fisherman sail. This current sail plan makes her profile distinct.

Life on the ocean goes back for generations in Capt. Dorr's family. Owen's grandfather was mate on the schooner *Edna Hoyt*, the last five-masted schooner in the world to sail. In the 1940s, Owen's parents sailed aboard the schooner *Enterprise* where his father was mate and his mother the cook. As a child, Owen spent his summers on Vinalhaven, the large island that divides east Penobscot Bay from west. The ocean was his backyard. There, he worked for local fishermen as well as on a variety of vessels in the windjammer fleet, including as mate on *Nathaniel Bowditch*. As Owen says, "It's easier to name a boat I haven't sailed on."

Before his schooner days, Owen's plan was to study marine architecture and design. But, after his first summer as crew on a windjammer, he was hooked. He earned his captain's license in 1989, and spent time traveling and sailing from Newfoundland to the West Indies, often

involved in shipboard educational programs. Cathie, together with her parents and sisters, came to the Maine coast in 1998 on a windjammer vacation. It was on that trip that the couple met, and the rest —as they say—is history.

Life aboard the *Bowditch* these days is a family affair. As hands-on owners and operators, their two sons sail with them. Early one beautiful morning at anchor last season, Cathie and Owen took the boys to nearby clam flats. While the couple dug clams for that afternoon's appetizer, the boys were gathering some pets. Once back on board, the boys proudly showed the guests their "pets for the morning," two hermit crabs. Recognizing that many guests are interested in an adult-only vacation, but that this is a great family vacation, they designate four or five trips for families with children ages five and up. The remaining trips are for adults and children 14 or older. But, these trips are not just for youngsters—Cathie's grandfather, who is in his 80's tries to make it up to Maine to sail with them once a season.

Owen's brother Paul is the ship's cook. Paul has been sailing for the past 25 years, working both on deck and in the galley. He fell in love with cooking 16 years ago aboard *Stephen Taber* and has honed his talents in many different galleys in the fleet. Cooking on a seasoned, authentic cast-iron stove, he prepares hearty New England fare, often with a twist. His travels and experiences have influenced his cooking, with dishes like African Ground-Nut Soup, Chicken Marbella, curries, and authentic Italian style polenta. He enjoys talking with guests about what they're eating and loves to create new recipes to augment his repertoire. He is occasionally joined in the galley by a Cuban friend who, as a guest chef, brings the flavors of black beans, pork, garlic, and citrus to the *Bowditch*'s menu. "Our families' influence shows up throughout the menu weekly," says Cathie in Betty's Blueberry Buckle, Grandma Jane's Chocolate Hermits, Aunt Marion's Blueberry Cake, and Mom's Quiche to name a few.

The hallmark of the *Bowditch*'s food is freshness and seasonality. On the brief turnarounds in port to unload as well as reload passengers and provisions, Cathie and Paul scour local farmers' markets for the season's best produce. Herbs used in the galley are grown in Owen and Cathie's garden, as well as in window boxes in the galley. Even the wonderful coffee served on board is locally roasted in Rockland, Maine, especially for the passengers of the *Bowditch*. The aroma of the "Bowditch Blend," freshly brewed throughout the day, greets guests as they enjoy a quiet morning at anchor. Or they might be sipping Bowditch Blend with a French Toast Soufflé topped with Maine maple syrup, or pancakes made with blueberries from Stockton Springs, Maine. Paul's signature hot fruit compote is another regular on the breakfast menu. Hand-churned ice cream perfectly accents a blueberry buckle or apple crisp. For guests who wish to bring their own beverages onboard, there is an

afternoon cocktail hour, with plenty of ice available.

A friend who cultivates oysters locally, occasionally joins the guests with a bucketful, coming aboard to demonstrate how to open oysters and, of course, to enjoy them with the passengers. Naturally, the lobster for the *Bowditch*'s island lobster bake comes from local fishermen. The night of the lobster bake is the cook's night off. Capt. Owen takes over to serve both passengers and crew. Owen and Cathie's signature flourishes for the lobster bakes are little touches like kosher hot dogs, kielbasa, salt potatoes, and dips with fresh veggies. The final treats—coming after the lobsters are devoured—are s'mores and fresh watermelon along with the captain's campfire coffee.

The importance of family aboard the *Bowditch* is evident in another significant way. Owen and Cathie, who both lost their mothers to breast cancer, are active supporters of breast cancer awareness and research. The ship's store is stocked with "pink" items (signifying breast cancer awareness) and the *Bowditch* hosts a couple of pink cruises each season. Money raised from these initiatives is donated to local and national groups. Cathie's mother, who was a nurse, founded a legacy program—The Compass Program—for breast cancer education for those newly diagnosed (find a link on the *Bowditch* website).

To the graceful waltz of the *Bowditch* there is time for every simple pleasure you've been missing: a lazy card game, a good yarn, an afternoon of bird watching, a night of glittering stars. For those inclined, guests can help in the operation of the vessel, learning about the traditional arts of sailing. Pair it all with fresh, hand-crafted food from the galley and your experience is complete.

ABOVE: Designed by a yacht designer, *Nathaniel Bowditch* has graceful lines for a schooner.

BELOW: Relax on deck or help with the sailing—it's your choice.

Nathaniel Bowditch
Captain Owen and Cathie Dorr
Length on deck: 82 feet
Length overall: 108 feet
Guests: 24
(207) 596-0401
(800) 288-4098
sailbowditch@verizon.net
www.windjammervacation.com

French Toast Soufflé

This can be prepared the night before, making it a perfect brunch dish.

6 eggs

4 cups milk or orange juice

2 teaspoons cinnamon

1 teaspoon nutmeg

1 tablespoon vanilla
extract

1 ½ cups sugar

1 stick melted butter

1 loaf Italian or French
bread, torn into large
pieces

SERVES 4-6

HOT FRUIT COMPOTE:

1 cup coarsely chopped or
small dried fruits
(prunes, apricots,
raisins, cranberries)

1 cup fresh fruit, such as
berries or chopped
apples, peaches, pears
or plums

½ cup sugar

1 cup orange juice

SERVES 4

Combine all of the ingredients except the bread and whisk until smooth. Add the bread pieces and stir to soak the bread. Cover and refrigerate at least one hour, or overnight.

Preheat the oven to 400 degrees. Lightly grease an 8x8-inch baking pan. Transfer the bread mixture to the prepared pan and cook for 35–45 minutes, until slightly puffed up and golden brown. Serve hot with real maple syrup or hot fruit compote.

For the hot fruit compote:
Combine all of the ingredients in a saucepan and simmer for 30 minutes, stirring occasionally. The compote can be made several days ahead and stored in the refrigerator. Reheat as needed.

Mom's Quiche

This has been part of Cathie's family's traditional Christmas brunch since she was a little girl. It works very well as a light dinner when served with a fresh salad.

Preheat the oven to 450 degrees. In a skillet over medium heat, sauté the leeks in the butter until tender, about 10 minutes.

Line the pie shell with layers of the spinach, mushrooms, leeks, and Swiss cheese.

In a bowl, whisk together the eggs, cream, and salt. Pour over the vegetables and cheese. Bake at 450 for about 10 minutes. Reduce heat to 325 degrees and bake until set, about 45 minutes.

1 tablespoon butter

1 cup washed, sliced leeks

1 unbaked 8 or 9-inch pie crust

1 cup coarsely chopped fresh spinach leaves

½ cup sliced mushrooms

2 cups shredded Swiss cheese

3 eggs

1 ½ cups cream

1 teaspoon salt, or to taste

Pinch of nutmeg

SERVES 4-6

Chili for a Crowd

This is served on deck with big soup mugs and lots of toppings: grated cheese, chopped onions, chopped hot or sweet peppers, avocado, sour cream, hot sauce— anything goes. A basket of hot cornbread and a crock of fresh butter, and you have a hearty meal for the masses.

4 tablespoons vegetable oil, more as needed

3 pounds chuck meat, cut into small (½-inch) cubes

2 cups chopped onion

2 cups chopped green pepper

2 jalapeno peppers, chopped

1 tablespoon ground cumin

2 tablespoons chili powder

1 teaspoon hot red pepper flakes

2 cans (28 ounces) crushed tomatoes

2 cans (28 ounce) kidney beans, with their liquid

Assorted condiments for serving (grated cheese, chopped onion, chopped hot or sweet peppers, diced avocado, sour cream, hot sauce, etc.)

SERVES 10-12

Heat 2 tablespoons of the oil in a large pot until quite hot. Sear the chuck meat in the hot oil in batches, removing the meat to a plate as it browns. Add more oil to the pot as needed. Once all of the meat has been browned and removed to the plate add the onions, peppers, and spices and cook until the onions are soft.

Add the meat back to the pot with the tomatoes and beans and simmer 2–3 hours, until the meat is fork tender. Serve with assorted condiments.

Ground-Nut Soup

This rich African-inspired soup makes use of peanuts—or "ground nuts"—as they are known in some parts of the world.

Heat the oil in a stock pot until quite hot. Brown the chicken on all sides and remove to a platter, leaving the oil behind in the pot. Add the onions and peppers and sauté until the vegetables are tender, about 5 minutes. Reduce heat if needed to avoid over browning.

Add the flour and cook for 2–3 minutes, stirring constantly.

Whisk in the chicken stock, bring to a boil, then reduce the heat and simmer for 5 minutes.

Add the remaining ingredients and whisk until smooth. Add the chicken thighs back to the soup and cook over medium-low heat at barely a simmer until the chicken is cooked through and almost falling off the bone, about 40 minutes. Serve the soup in large bowls, with a chicken thigh in each bowl. Garnish with chopped peanuts or diced red pepper.

1 tablespoon olive oil, more as needed

6 chicken thighs, boneless and skinless if desired

1 cup chopped onion

1 cup chopped red pepper

2 tablespoons flour

4 cups chicken stock

1 cup smooth, unsalted peanut butter

1 cup heavy cream

2 teaspoons ground red pepper

1 teaspoon turmeric

Salt and black pepper, to taste

SERVES 6

Chicken Marbella

This is a beautiful and aromatic dish that can easily be expanded to feed a larger crowd. It is just as delicious the next day.

8-12 chicken pieces, thighs, drumsticks, and split breasts

4 cups red wine

7 tablespoons olive oil, divided

1 cup sliced red onion

2 teaspoons minced fresh thyme

Coarse salt, to taste

Black pepper, to taste

2 cups small whole white mushrooms

2 tablespoons flour

1 ½ cups large pitted prunes

1 ½ cups stuffed green olives

POLENTA

4 cups water

1 teaspoon salt

1 cup yellow cornmeal

½ cup grated Parmesan cheese

4 tablespoons butter

SERVES 4-6

Combine the red wine, 4 tablespoons of the olive oil, red onion, and thyme in a large non-reactive bowl. Marinate the chicken overnight, or for at least 4 hours, in the refrigerator. Remove the chicken from the marinade. Strain the marinade and set aside, discarding the solids.

Pat the chicken dry and sprinkle on all sides with salt and pepper. Heat the remaining 3 tablespoons of olive oil in a large, deep skillet. Sauté the mushrooms in the hot oil until browned. Remove the mushrooms, leaving behind any oil.

Sear the chicken in the skillet until browned on all sides. Remove the chicken from the pan, leaving behind any oil and drippings.

Whisk the flour into the drippings and cook 2 to 3 minutes. Whisk the strained marinade into the flour. Bring to a boil and add the chicken, mushrooms, prunes, and olives. Simmer for 20 minutes, or until chicken is cooked through. Remove the chicken to a serving platter and keep warm. Continue to simmer the sauce until it has thickened to a gravy-like consistency. Serve over rice, polenta, or egg noodles.

Polenta

Captain Owen's brother, Paul, the cook aboard the *Bowditch* first tasted polenta at an Italian friend's house as a boy. When he referred to it "cornmeal mush," he was quickly corrected!

Bring the water to a boil. Add the salt. Slowly pour in the cornmeal, whisking constantly to prevent lumps. Reduce heat and cook, stirring constantly, until thick, about 20 minutes. Stir in the cheese and butter. Serve immediately.

Stephen Taber

CAPTAIN NOAH BARNES has some happy passengers aboard. They have come for one of *Stephen Taber*'s wonderful wine cruises. In this instance, Noah's wife—Jane—is aboard, bringing guests a wealth of knowledge about wines, cheeses, and food pairings, drawn from years of experience in the wine industry. Although very knowledgeable about wine, Noah and Jane are far from wine snobs. Finding a good wine is all about individual tastes. As Jane says, "If you think it tastes good, it is good!" And the camaraderie that develops while sipping wines makes it easy to make new friends.

Although Noah has traveled widely and sailed in many parts of the world, he considers the Maine coast home. He grew up sailing with his parents, Ellen and Ken Barnes, former owners of the *Taber*. "Sailing the Maine coast is unparalleled. It's challenging and rewarding and just an intrinsically good experience," Noah says. "We think the food aesthetic should match our surroundings."

Serving good food on the *Taber* is a tradition begun by Ellen, who made it her goal in the late 1970s to elevate the quality of the onboard food. Noah's family grew their own herbs, began making breads and

pastries from scratch, and became known for the quality of the *Taber*'s food, which has been featured in the *Boston Globe*, the *New York Times*, and on the *Food Network*.

A typical menu might feature artisanal cheese, hand-rolled gnocchi, osso buco, or a lasagna with venison ragu. Admits Noah, "We go a bit crazy with hors d'oeuvres." You might find hand-rolled sushi, duck confit blintzes, or artichokes with buerre blanc to enjoy with a pre-dinner drink or glass of wine. And, as is customary aboard other Maine windjammers, the *Taber*'s passengers can expect an all-you-can-eat island Lobster Bake. Noah explains that he doesn't have a food budget—"We'll go to just about any lengths to educate and entertain our guests."

Noah may be serious about food and his schooner, but that's about it. He likes to have fun and wants his guests to enjoy their time at sea. You might find yourself in the middle of a marshmallow war, with guests and crew using slingshots to bombard other schooners. "The good-natured joking and camaraderie within the fleet is what makes this such a wonderful community," Noah says.

Although there are only four official wine cruises per season, guests can sip the

TOP: *Stephen Taber* was built as a working schooner, but her pleasing lines also caught the eye of yachtsmen.

ABOVE: Hand-rolled sushi aboard the *Taber*.

house wines most nights on any voyage. Ellen still trains the chefs (Noah and Jane are careful to point out that they have "chefs in the galley, not cooks") who are on a mission to serve up "hearty, tasty, soulful food. A great meal that makes you want to get up and dance." And you might well want to do just that when the musicians aboard begin to play, later in the evening. On board, you might find guitars, a Norwegian folk fiddle, harmonicas, mandolins, an acoustic bass, and hand drums.

But the *Stephen Taber* is not just about food and wine. Known in the Maine windjammer fleet as the "Good Luck Ship," the vessel has an incredibly rich history. Launched in 1871, she is one of the oldest documented sailing vessels in the United States, and has been honored by inclusion on the National Register of Historic Places. As a cargo-carrying coasting schooner, with an overall length of 115 feet and 68 feet on deck, she plied the waters of New York Harbor captained by Byron G. Halleck until 1899, when a tugboat captain misjudged the tricky currents of the aptly named Hell's Gate and damaged the *Taber*. The

captain made full reparations, and Byron decided to use the windfall to repair and upgrade the *Taber*. This was something of a gamble, as sailing vessels increasingly were being replaced by steam-powered boats.

But the move paid off. Shortly after her refitting, her graceful lines caught the eye of a wealthy family from Long Island who decided the *Taber* would make the perfect floating summer home. It was a leisurely life for the hardworking schooner. The family installed "facilities for the ladies" in the forward hold, and moved aboard with their servants, chefs, rocking chairs, and linens. It was quite a step up in society, and eventually the *Taber* fell in with the elegant yachts of the New York Yacht Club and traveled between Long Island and Newport, Rhode Island, until 1902, still with Captain Byron at the helm.

But the *Taber*'s new identity must not have suited her captain. After a few seasons with the posh yachting set, he returned the ship to her former hardworking duties; hauling cordwood, coal, and other cargos, until 1920 when Byron came ashore for good.

In 1929, the *Taber* lay in Brooksville, Maine, with only a handful of coasting schooners still afloat. Enter Captain Fred Wood, who also gambled on the sturdy and nimble vessel. This time, though, there was no windfall to rebuild the boat and very little money to be found anywhere, with the Depression haunting the country. So Fred undertook the project and rebuilt the *Taber* himself. She was again reincarnated.

Fast-forward to 1979. Captain Noah's father, Ken, surveyed the once-again neglected schooner that was swinging on a mooring in Camden Harbor, Maine. As Ken has said often, "I'd never been much for love at first sight, but I knew enough to recognize it when it struck." Ellen was just as enchanted. Like the *Taber*'s previous owners, they were willing to do whatever it took to bring her back to tip-top condition. And she has stayed that way, having been in the Barnes family ever since.

When Ken and Ellen decided to retire, Noah was leading the life of a well-heeled young professional in Manhattan. His parents asked if he wanted to take over the *Taber* and gave him six weeks to decide. In a bold and life-changing move, he and then-girlfriend Jane Barrett took the plunge. Describing herself as a "bona fide landlubber," Jane hardly could have imagined that she would one day be the co-owner of the floating historic landmark that is the *Stephen Taber*.

Noah and Jane were married in Camden in 2005 and sail together as often as possible, although Jane—when not acting as wine expert and chief morale officer—still is active in her career in the wine business. Jane works with Terlato Wines International on a portfolio including Gaja, Michel Chapoutier, and Champagne Bollinger, which you may get to taste on one of the *Taber*'s wine cruises, perhaps paired with the classic French savory puff pastries known as gougères. (See the recipe on page 133.)

The *Taber* also hosts photography and lighthouse cruises in addition to the traditional gatherings of the Maine fleet, such as the Great Schooner Race and the Schooner Gam. Like the other captains in the Maine windjammer fleet, being at the helm of the *Taber* is far more than a job. In Noah and Jane's case, it's about creating a feeling of family on board and caring for a quintessential part of maritime history.

BELOW: Happiness is a great breakfast.

BOTTOM: Ready for a wine tasting.

WINE AND CHEESE ABOARD THE *TABER*

CRUISES ABOARD *Stephen Taber* generally include at least one cheese tasting, generally offered before dinner as the hors d'oeuvres course. Cheeses are an important part of the menu on other occasions as well. Their gorgeous cheese displays will often include cured or smoked meats, pâtés, fruits, and nuts, along with mild crackers or sliced baguettes, all designed to let the flavor of each cheese shine through. Their cheese offerings are as eclectic as their wines, showcasing artisanal cheeses from nearby Maine farms, small European farmhouse producers and as far afield as King Island, a remote island in the Bass Strait located between Australia and Tasmania.

Jane and Noah take special care with the cheeses they select to complement their wines. Working closely with Sage Market in Rockland, they are able to get recommendations about great local choices like Stonington Granite, a goat cheese produced in small batches by Sunset Acres Farm and Dairy in Brooksville, Maine.

Jane recommends starting out with milder cheeses, like young chèvres or Bries and progressing to stronger, more aged cheeses like cheddars and Goudas. "Then try moving on to something like a Tallegio, Morbier or aged Camembert." The blue cheeses are last in the lineup, and often include a favorite of Jane and Noah's, the delicious Bayley Hazen Blue, a natural rind raw cow's milk blue cheese produced by Jasper Hill Farm in Greensboro, Vermont. Share your favorites with Jane and Noah. They love trying new things.

Stephen Taber

Captain Noah and Jane Barnes
Length on deck: 68 feet
Length overall: 115 feet
Guests: 22
(207) 594-0035
(800) 999-7352
info@stephentaber.com
www.mainewindjammers.com

Granola

The *Taber*'s classic granola recipe has been handed down from Captain Noah's mom, Ellen, who cooked aboard the *Taber* before Noah and Jane took over. Ellen still serves it at their historic inn, The Captain Lindsey House, in Rockland, Maine. It's a hearty start to a great day on the water.

¾ cup honey

¾ cup oil

2 teaspoons vanilla

4 cups rolled oats

2 cups bran buds

1 ½ cups shredded coconut

1 ½ cups chopped walnuts

MAKES ABOUT 8 CUPS

Preheat the oven to 300 degrees. Heat the honey, oil, and vanilla in a small pot over low heat.

In a large bowl, mix together the dry ingredients. Pour the warm honey mixture evenly over the dry ingredients and toss well to combine.

Spread the granola evenly over two baking sheets and bake at 300 degrees for 15-20 minutes, stirring every 5 minutes or so until lightly browned. Cool completely and store in an airtight container for several weeks.

Gougères

The chef aboard the *Taber* makes these classic French savory pastries during the wine cruises. They are the perfect hors d'oeuvres with Champagne Bollinger.

Preheat the oven to 375 degrees. Bring the water to a boil in a saucepan with the butter, salt, and sugar.

Add the flour and stir vigorously until the dough becomes a ball and pulls from the edges of the pot. Remove to a mixing bowl.

While the mixture is still hot, beat in the eggs, one at a time, mixing until completely combined after each addition.

Add the Gruyère, ½ cup of the Parmesan, the mustard, and the cayenne and mix well.

Drop small spoonfuls onto a buttered baking sheet and sprinkle the reserved Parmesan over the top of the gougères. Bake at 375 degrees for 25–30 minutes, or until puffy, golden, and crisp. Serve warm with your favorite wine.

1 cup water

½ cup butter

1 tablespoon salt

½ teaspoon sugar

1 cup flour

4 eggs

¾ cup shredded Gruyère or other Swiss-style cheese

¾ cup shredded aged Parmesan or Asiago

1 teaspoon dry mustard

Pinch of cayenne

MAKES 5 DOZEN

Citrus Cilantro Salmon and Pineapple Mango Salsa

4 each boneless, skinless salmon
    filets (6-8 ounces per filet)

2 tablespoons fresh lemon juice

1 tablespoon minced garlic

2 tablespoons minced fresh cilantro

Salt and pepper, to taste

2 tablespoons olive oil

SERVES 4

PINEAPPLE MANGO SALSA:

1 cup diced pineapple

½ cup diced mango

2 tablespoons finely diced red onion

2 tablespoons finely diced tomato

½ teaspoon minced garlic

½ teaspoon minced fresh ginger

1 tablespoon minced fresh cilantro

¼ teaspoon crushed red pepper
    flakes (more if you like)

1 tablespoon lime juice

2 tablespoons olive oil

Salt and black pepper, to taste

SERVES 4

With just a hint of garlic, citrus, and herbs, fresh salmon shines in this signature dish aboard the *Stephen Taber*.

Preheat the oven to 400 degrees. Arrange the salmon filets on a lightly greased baking sheet or roasting pan. Drizzle the filets with the lemon juice. Rub the garlic, cilantro, salt, and pepper over each filet. Drizzle with the olive oil and bake at 400 degrees for 15–20 minutes, until salmon is just cooked through. Serve with Pineapple Mango Salsa.

Pineapple Mango Salsa

This beautifully balanced tropical salsa is the perfect accompaniment to the *Taber*'s Citrus Cilantro Salmon.

Combine all of the ingredients in a bowl and mix well. Chill before serving.

Tuscan Beef

This recipe is from Jane's sister, Elizabeth Fanneron. Jane made it for Noah on his birthday a few years ago and it's been a favorite on the *Taber* ever since. You can save time by asking your butcher to butterfly the London Broil for you.

2-3 pounds London Broil

6 tablespoons olive oil

½ cup red wine

2 tablespoons red wine vinegar

2 tablespoons minced garlic

1 tablespoon minced fresh parsley

1 teaspoon fresh cracked pepper, more to taste

6 thin slices prosciutto

2 tablespoons minced shallots sautéed in butter

1 cup grated Parmesan cheese

1 cup sliced roasted red peppers

¼ cup chiffonade basil leaves

Salt, to taste

SERVES 4-6

Place the London Broil in a non-reactive roasting pan. Mix together 4 tablespoons of the olive oil, red wine, red wine vinegar, 1 tablespoon garlic, parsley, and cracked pepper. Pour the mixture over the London Broil and marinate, refrigerated, for several hours or overnight.

Preheat the oven to 375 degrees. Remove the meat from the marinade, reserve the marinade, and butterfly the beef. Pound lightly until the meat is about ¼-½ inch thick.

Arrange the prosciutto over the butterflied meat. Spread the shallots, Parmesan, roasted peppers, and basil over the prosciutto. Roll the meat into a tight roulade and tie with twine. Sprinkle the beef all over with salt and cracked pepper.

In a skillet, heat the remaining olive oil until it is almost smoking. Sear the roulade on all sides. Transfer to a roasting pan and pour the reserved marinade over the roulade.

Roast at 375 for 45 minutes to 1 hour, until the meat reaches an internal temperature of 145–160 degrees (medium rare to medium). Transfer the beef to a cutting board and let rest 10 minutes. Prepare a pan sauce with the drippings, if you like. Slice beef and arrange on a platter or on individual dinner plates, accompanied by roasted potatoes and a vegetable.

Almond Tosca Bars

These rich bar cookies are often served after lunch with fresh fruit, making for delicious finger food while underway.

Preheat the oven to 350 degrees. Combine all ingredients for the bars, except the chocolate pieces. Pat into an 8×8-inch baking pan and bake at 350 degrees for 12 minutes.

Remove the pan from the oven and sprinkle the chocolate pieces over the top. Let them melt, then spread evenly. Set the pan aside while you prepare the topping, but keep the oven at 350 degrees.

In a saucepan, combine all of the ingredients for the topping and boil for 3 minutes. Pour over the chocolate and bake the bars for another 12–15 minutes, until lightly browned. Cool completely before cutting into bars.

For the bars:

1 ¼ cups flour

½ teaspoon salt

⅓ cup sugar

⅓ cup butter

1 teaspoon grated lemon peel

½ cup semisweet chocolate pieces

For the topping:

¾ cup chopped almonds

½ cup sugar

⅓ cup light cream

½ stick butter

MAKES ABOUT 16 BARS

Victory Chimes

ALTHOUGH *VICTORY CHIMES* has become an icon of the Maine coast, *Edwin & Maud*—as *Victory Chimes* was originally christened—was launched in 1900 from Bethel, Delaware.

Designed to haul lumber along the east coast, *Victory Chimes* was one of thirty schooners built between the 1880s and 1920s by J. M. C. Moore and George K. Phillips. Their Bethel shipyard was located along a narrow bend in the Nanticoke River that emptied into the Chesapeake Bay. *Victory Chimes* was designed with the Chesapeake & Delaware Canal in mind. Her hull was wall-sided—or nearly perpendicular to the water—in order to maximize cargo space. Utilizing a centerboard, she drew less than 8 feet of water, which allowed her to navigate the shallow waters of Chesapeake Bay.

Adaptability has allowed *Victory Chimes* to survive and leave her mark on American maritime history. A merchant vessel during both world wars, her captain reported on the status of the anti-submarine minefields off the Chesapeake Bay during World War II, checking for mines that had broken loose. After the war ended, a Baltimore and Ohio Railroad man named Herman Knurst had a vision. In 1946, he purchased

Edwin & Maud from the C. C. Paul Fleet in Baltimore, Maryland; built cabins in the cargo hold, and converted her to a "dude cruiser." She became a mainstay in Herman's Chesapeake Bay Vacation Cruises sailing out of Annapolis, Maryland.

In 1954, *Edwin & Maud* caught the eye of Captain Frederick Boyd Guild of Castine, Maine. He sailed her north and renamed her *Victory Chimes*. Then, after thirty years of windjamming along the coast of Maine and endearing herself to a second region of the Atlantic seaboard, it was time for the schooner to adapt once again. Captain Frederick, approaching retirement, sold the vessel to two businessmen from Duluth, Minnesota. *Victory Chimes* was towed to the Great Lakes, via the Saint Lawrence Seaway for a brief stay before the vessel fell upon hard times.

In 1987, *Victory Chimes* was purchased by Tom Monaghan, owner of Domino's Pizza and the Detroit Tigers baseball team. Tom financed a major restoration to the tune of $1.5 million. Captain Paul DeGaeta, who at the time was fleet captain for Domino's Pizza Marine Division, hired Captain Kip Files to oversee the restoration. Domino's—which had changed the vessel's name once again (this time to *Domino Effect*)—eventu-

TOP: Anchored in a quiet harbor or under sail, *Victory Chimes*'s three masts make her immediately recognizable.

"She's always been a working vessel," Captain Kip says. "She has never had a dime of public money or foundation money. In this day and age, for a vessel this large, that is an incredible accomplishment. Paul and I are very proud of that."

In fall 1999, the captains sailed in the Great Chesapeake Bay Schooner Race and *Victory Chimes* wintered at the Chesapeake Bay Maritime Museum. The year 2000 marked the one hundredth birthday of *Victory Chimes*, and the captains decided to bring the vessel to her home bay and celebrate by opening *Victory Chimes* to the public. Captain Paul and his family were aboard on the last night of the twentieth century.

Her roots may be in the Chesapeake, but *Victory Chimes* has become one of the enduring symbols of the Maine coast. In 2002, the people of Maine voted on four designs for the state quarter. The chosen design originated with a family in Rockland and features *Victory Chimes* sailing by the Pemaquid Point lighthouse in Bristol, Maine. The quarter was released by the U.S. Mint in 2003.

At 132 feet on deck (172 overall), *Victory Chimes* is the largest vessel in the Maine windjammer fleet, allowing plenty of room for anyone who wants to stretch and relax on one of the overstuffed deck mats. Most cabins are doubles, but there are single cabins and larger ones that can accommodate a family. Four suites are available for special occasions or for those who want a bit more luxury. Each has a double bed, a head, and stocked bookshelves (including a collection of Maine's favorite horror author Stephen King). The Governor's Suite earned that moniker after former Maine Governor Angus King slept there.

Sailors are a superstitious lot, and the

ally placed the vessel for sale. Kip and Paul were charged with selling the ship.

It seemed that *Victory Chimes* was destined to leave U.S. waters forever, as a Japanese company was interested in buying her to turn the historic schooner into a restaurant. But, Kip and Paul were troubled by this. As Paul says, "We couldn't bear the idea that this American nautical treasure would be leaving her native waters for good."

So Kip and Paul did a little adapting on their own: they purchased *Domino Effect*. Their first official act was to change her name back to *Victory Chimes*.

For a hardworking ram schooner, 15 years of sailing was considered a successful run. But 108 years at work proves *Victory Chimes* was able to adapt to changes in markets and the way she made a living. Captains Kip and Paul consider themselves caretakers and are proud that *Victory Chimes* received National Historic Landmark status in 1997, on their watch. She is the largest passenger-carrying sailing vessel under the American flag. *Victory Chimes* is also the last three-masted or larger vessel built during America's golden age of sail that is still sailing.

onboard food isn't exempt. A knife sticking out of a loaf of bread meant a fight would break out. A loaf left upside down foretold a shipwreck. If every bit of food was eaten at mealtime, it foretold fair weather. And, if this last legend is true, *Victory Chimes* should encounter lots of fair weather, as hearty appetites seem to come with the sea air.

Cooking aboard any vessel presents unique challenges. The adaptability that marked the ship's history also has been a hallmark of her galley and her cooks for more than half a century sailing the Maine coast. For a full passenger load including crew, the cook and two galley assistants produce fifty meals a sitting. Everything is made from scratch, using a twin-oven, cast-iron stove.

Food aboard *Victory Chimes* is plentiful, traditional, and tasty—whether it's breakfast, lunch, or dinner. There is always the Lobster Dinner on one night of each cruise (with alternatives provided for those who are not seafood eaters). Breakfast and dinner are served below decks in the spacious saloon, but guests and crew often gather on deck to toast the day's adventures after the anchor is dropped. Lunch generally is served on deck, as the ship likely is to be under way at that hour.

Ship's cook Mary Walker retired in 1996 after six years in *Victory Chimes*'s galley. Many of Mary's traditional recipes were compiled by Mary and Captain Paul (no slouch in the galley himself) in the *Victory Chimes Cookbook*, which is in its third edition. Also included are recipes from family, friends, passengers, and crew. Mary made a point to search for recipes that might have been found aboard ships at the turn of the century, food that tastes "like Grandma used to make," as Mary says in the cookbook's preface.

The recipes below are some of the classic dishes still served and still cooked on the *Victory Chimes*'s old woodstove, or, as Mary called it, "the old black stove."

Current ship's cook Pam Sheridan has been aboard for seven years and is another passenger favorite. As do all ship's cooks, Pam has to take into consideration a number of variables when preparing meals: the motion of the boat, the vagaries of cooking on a wood-fired stove, the weather, the supply of perishable foods, as well as the experience and expertise of her helpers in the galley.

The signature farewell breakfast on the last day of the cruise is classic Eggs Benedict, but other specialties include blueberry pancakes, a puffy cheese and egg bake, homemade granola, and a variety of breads and muffins. Lunches often feature hearty soups and chowders (Pam laughingly handed over the recipe for Cheeseburger Soup—a.k.a. Heart Attack in a Bowl), as well as salads and breads. Dinner might be Yankee pot roast, chicken pot pie, or roast turkey—all served with delicious sides. And be sure to leave room for dessert like Alotta Chocolate, made with two types of chocolate and a dash of Kahlua or Grand Marnier.

ABOVE: Salt air and sunshine result in big smiles.

BELOW: A peaceful cove.

BELOW LEFT: The sun sets behind the *Victory Chimes*.

Victory Chimes
Captains Kip Files and
  Paul DeGaeta
Length on deck: 132 feet
Length overall: 172 feet
Guests: 40
(800) 745-5651
kipfiles@gwi.net
www.victorychimes.com

Eggs Benedict

This traditional brunch dish is always served on the last day of the *Victory Chimes*' cruises as a special farewell to their guests.

4 English muffins, split
   and toasted

8 slices Canadian bacon or
   thinly sliced ham,
   heated

8 eggs

2 ½ cups hollandaise
   sauce

SERVES 4

HOLLANDAISE SAUCE:

3 sticks butter

6 egg yolks

3 tablespoons lemon juice

Salt, pepper,
   Worcestershire,
   and hot sauce to taste

MAKES ABOUT
   2 ½ CUPS

Heat the oven to 170 degrees. Have ready a freshly made batch of hollandaise sauce. Set out 4 dinner plates and place 2 English muffin halves, cut side up, on each plate. Place 1 slice of Canadian bacon on each muffin half and set the plates in the oven to keep warm.

Poach the eggs, 2 or 3 at a time, placing a poached egg on each muffin half as they are done. Keep the plates in the oven as you go along. Once all of the eggs have been poached and placed on an English muffin, ladle about 2 tablespoons of hollandaise sauce over each egg. Serve immediately.

Hollandaise Sauce

Heat the butter until it begins to bubble, but do not let it brown.

Place the yolks and lemon juice in the blender and process, covered, until smooth. With the blender running, drizzle in the hot butter until completely incorporated and the mixture is smooth, thick, and pale yellow. Season to taste with salt, pepper, Worcestershire, and hot sauce.

Pumpkin Yeast Bread

This loaf is yeast risen, giving it a lighter texture than traditional pumpkin breads.

2 teaspoons dry yeast

½ cup warm water

1 cup pumpkin puree

⅓ cup sugar

⅓ cup butter, melted

1 egg

1 teaspoon salt

3 cups flour, more as
    needed

MAKES 1 LOAF

Dissolve the yeast in the warm water and let set 10 minutes, until the mixture begins to froth.

Add the pumpkin puree, sugar, butter, egg, and salt and mix well.

Add the flour and mix to form a dough. Turn onto a lightly floured surface and knead until smooth, adding more flour as needed if the dough is too sticky. Place the dough in a greased bowl, cover with a clean cloth and let rise until doubled in size.

Grease a 9×5×2½-inch loaf pan. Punch down the dough, form into a loaf, and place in the prepared pan. Cover and let rise until doubled in size.

Preheat oven to 350 degrees and bake for 30–40 minutes, until the bread is golden brown and cooked through. Let cool for 10 minutes in the pan, then run a knife around the edge and remove the bread to a wire rack to cool completely.

Broccoli-Cauliflower Salad

Serve this alongside the Cheeseburger Soup for a crunchy and nutritious salad that can be made ahead of time. If you'd prefer a less crunchy texture, you could blanch the broccoli and cauliflower beforehand and chill.

In a large bowl, combine all ingredients except tomatoes. Marinate overnight in the refrigerator. Just before serving, add the cherry tomatoes and toss to combine.

1 head of broccoli, cut into bite-sized florets

1 head of cauliflower, cut into bite-sized florets

1 ½ cups sliced, pitted black olives

½ cup diced onion

1 can (8-ounce) water chestnuts

1 cup Italian vinaigrette dressing, more if needed

Salt and pepper, to taste

1 pint cherry tomatoes, halved

SERVES 4-6

Cheeseburger Soup

1 pound ground beef

1 tablespoon olive oil

1 tablespoon butter

1 cup finely chopped onion

2 teaspoons minced garlic

1 jalapeno pepper, minced

2 tablespoons mustard
   seed

1 teaspoon Kitchen
   Bouquet or liquid
   smoke

2 pounds Velveta cheese

2 cups evaporated milk

2 cubes beef bouillon

Salt and pepper to taste

SERVES 4-6

This signature *Victory Chimes* soup is lovingly referred to by the crew as "Heart Attack in a Bowl." It may not be low fat, but it's a hearty favorite.

In a large pot, brown the beef in the olive oil and butter. Add the onions, garlic, and jalapeno and cook until the onions are soft.

Stir in the mustard seed and Kitchen Bouquet, then lay the American cheese over the ground beef. Allow the cheese to melt for a couple of minutes. Add the evaporated milk and beef bouillon, stir to combine, then cook at a bare simmer for about 10 minutes. Season to taste with salt and pepper and serve immediately.

Alotta Chocolate

The balance of semi-sweet and darker bittersweet chocolates are rounded out with a dash of your favorite liqueur.

In a sauce pan, heat the milk with the sugar and the chocolate, whisking until smooth.

Whisk in the eggs, salt, and liqueur. Pour into 6–8 individual serving cups or into a large serving dish, and refrigerate for about an hour, until set. Serve with fresh whipped cream.

1 ½ cups milk

¼ cup scant sugar

6 ounces semi-sweet chocolate

8 ounces bittersweet chocolate

2 eggs, beaten

Pinch of salt

2 tablespoons Kahlua, Grand Marnier, or other favorite liqueur.

SERVES 6-8

Terminology

A

About: To pass from one tack to the opposite one.

Adrift: Broken loose, as a boat from her moorings.

Amidships: In or toward the middle of a ship in regard to length or breadth.

Astern: The bearing of an object 180 degrees from ahead.

B

Beam: The width of a boat at its widest part.

Becalmed: Having no wind to fill the sails.

Belay: To secure a line to a cleat or pin.

Bend: To make fast; also, a kind of knot.

Berth: A bed or bunk, usually built in, a slip or docking space for a vessel.

Bight: The noose or slack part of a rope between the ends.

Bilge: Lowest part of the boat's interior.

Bitts: Upright pieces of timber to which lines are belayed.

Blocks: Contrivances with sheaves or pulleys, used to lead lines advantageously.

Bobstay: A chain or line from the waterline to the bowsprit end to sustain it.

Boom: The spar extending from the mast to hold or extend the foot of a sail.

Bow: The front, or "pointy end" of the vessel.

Bowsprit: A spar extending forward from the stem of a vessel, usually for the purpose of carrying sail farther forward.

Bulkhead: Partitions dividing a ship into various compartments.

Buoy: A floating beacon.

C

Cabin: Sleeping quarters, usually with a door.

Can: A green buoy with a cylindrical top found on the port side when entering a channel.

Capsize: To turn over.

Cast off: To untie; to allow to go free.

Cat's paw: A light current of air seen rippling on the water.

Caulk: To fill the seams between planks with cotton or oakum.

Centerboard: An adjustable keel that drops through a slot in the bottom of a boat to provide ballast and sailing stability.

Cleat: A piece of wood or metal with two horns, upon which lines are secured.

Close hauled: Sailing as near as possible to the wind.

Coil: To gather a rope into circular rings one on another.

Companionway: The entryway to a cabin or compartment.

Course: The point of a compass on which a vessel sails; the direction she is going.

D

Davits: Bent iron stanchions extending over the side or stern, to which boats are hoisted.

Draft (Draught): The depth of a vessel below the waterline. Also a pleasurable libation frequently responsible for the necessity of a wardrobe "refit."

E

Ease off: To slacken

F

Fall off: To move away from the wind.

Fathom: A nautical measure of six feet.

Fiddle: An edging on tables, counter tops, and other furniture to hold items in place while the boat is in motion.

Forward: Toward the bow of the boat.

Foul: To come into a collision, an entangled sail or line.

Furl: To gather up and secure a sail or awning.

G

Gaff: The spar that supports the head of a fore-and-aft sail.

Gasket: A lashing of line or canvas used to secure furled sails, etc.

Galley: The nautical term for kitchen.

Gam: Vessels tied together for a visit and friendly get-together.

Gear: The general name for ropes, blocks, and tackles, etc.

Gimbaled: Pivoted or suspended to remain in an upright position, as a "gimbaled compass," a "gimbaled lamp," etc.

Go about: To change from one tack to the other by putting the helm down.

Gybe (also, "Jibe"): To pass the mainsail from one quarter to the other when running.

H

Halyards: The lines used to hoist sails.

Hard alee: The command that brings the vessel through the wind onto the opposite tack.

Hatch: An opening in the deck, leading below or providing ventilation.

Head: The nautical term for bathroom. So called because on early sailing ships it was located at the bow or head of the vessel.

Heave-to: To stop a vessel's way by so arranging the sails that she will lie nearly head to the wind and have no tendency to forge ahead.

Heeling: Inclining to one side.

Helm: The steering wheel or tiller of the boat.

Hoist away: An order to haul up.

Hull: The body of the vessel.

J

Jib: A triangular sail set on the bowsprit or jibboom.

K

Keel: The part of the vessel in the water and upon which all the rest is erected.

Knot: One nautical mile per hour. Originally measured with a fourteen second "sand glass" while counting the number of knots on a trailing line that slipped by the rail of the vessel.

L

LOA: "Length over all" or the overall length of the vessel

Lazaret: A storeroom or compartment.

Lee: The side sheltered from the wind.

Leeway: The drift of a vessel caused by the wind or tide.

Line: A rope with a specific purpose aboard a vessel.

Locker: Cupboard for storage.

Log: The record of a vessel's performance.

M

Mainsheet: A line by which the mainsail is hauled in or eased out.

Mainsail: A sail with its luff (forward edge) attached to the mainmast.

Mast: A vertical spar supporting booms, gaff and sails.

Mooring buoy: A buoy fitted with a ring and used for mooring a boat.

Moorings: The place where a vessel is usually kept when at anchor.

Monkey's Fist: A particular style of knot, spherical in shape, worked into the end of a heaving line.

N

Nun buoy: A red buoy with a conical top found on the starboard hand on entering a channel.

P

Painter: A line attached to the bow of a boat, by which she may be secured.

Pay-off: To recede from the wind, as a boat when the jib is hauled to windward and the main boom is eased off.

Peak-up: To elevate the aft end of a sail or gaff.

Port side: Left-hand side of the boat, looking forward from the stern.

Pullman: A single bunk with no door, curtained off.

R

Reef: To reduce sail by means of reef points.

Refit: The nautical equivalent of renovation of a vessel.

Rig: The combination of masts, booms, standing and running rigging and sails that propel a sailing craft.

Rudder: The flat blade that swings from side to side under water and is used to steer the boat.

Rules of the road: Regulations enacted for safety.

Running rigging: Those lines that reeve or lead through blocks and fair leads; includes halyards, sheets, downhauls, etc.

S

Saloon: The central cabin in the vessel, where dining occurs.

Schooner: Vessel with two or more masts, with the after mast as tall or taller than the other(s).

Scud: Run before the wind.

Sea anchor: A drag (drogue) thrown over the bow to hold the boat into the wind and sea.

Settee: Built-in bench, usually with cushions, for dining, either on deck or below.

Sheet: The line attached to the clew of a fore-and-aft sail by which it is held and worked.

Shrouds: Wire line used to support the mast on port and starboard.

Skipper: The captain or operator of a vessel.

Slack: The part of a line that hangs loose; allow to ease off. Also, the state of the tide when there is no horizontal motion.

Spill: To throw the wind out of a sail by easing the sheet or otherwise.

Splice: To join two ropes together by tucking ends.

Standing rigging: The lines that are stationary or seldom require alteration, such as shrouds and stays.

Starboard: The side to the right, looking forward.

Stay: Any line to support masts, fore and aft.

Stem: The timber at the extreme forward part of the boat, secured to the forward end of the keel, and supporting the bow planks.

Stern: The after or rear section of the ship.

T

Tack: The lower forward corner of a fore-and-aft sail. Close-hauled on the wind. To change from one tack to the other by putting the helm down and adjusting sails.

Tacking: Advancing by a series of zigzag courses towards the wind's eye.

Tackle: An arrangement of ropes and blocks to give a mechanical advantage.

Tiller: A (usually) curved and tapered stick that connects to the rudderstock, that is used for steering the boat.

Topsail: A three-sided sail that sets above a gaff; a four-sided sail whose head (upper edge) attaches to the yard of a topsail schooner.

U

Under way: A boat is under way when moving ahead.

W

Wake: The track left by a vessel on the water.

Waterline: The line painted on the side of a boat at the water's edge to indicate the proper trim.

Weigh the anchor: To raise the anchor and get it aboard.

Windjammer: A sailing ship; also, one of its crew.

Y

Yawl boat: A small, open, engine-driven boat that services an unpowered sailing vessel.

Courtesy of Maine Windjammer Cruises

Photo Credits

Many thanks to all who supplied photography for *Windjammer Cooking*.

Dave Aldrich, page 17

Joshua Barratt, pages 101, 106, 141

Dudley Bierau, page 23

Jan Burnham, page 104

Wendy Carlson, pages 2, 135

Paul Dorr, pages 124, 127, back cover

Jim Dugan, pages 90, 91

George Evans, page 61

Irv Green, page 31

Jeff Greenberg, pages 30, 61

Charles and Tom Greiner, page 81

Barbara Hatch, pages 50, 98

Annie Higbee, page 68

George Kovarik, page 58

Fred LeBlanc, cover, pages 5, 8, 14, 16, 24, 28, 30, 31, 33, 38, 41, 48, 51, 60, 63, 78, 100, 108, 110, 111, 118, 120, 121, 128, 130, 138

Captain Doug Lee, page 76

David Liscio, page 31

Margaret Liss, page 101

Meg Maiden, page 42

Captain Jen Martin, pages 18, 90, 95, 96, 97, back cover

Nancy Nevitt, page 101

Neal Parent, pages 21, 88, 91

Jean Pothier, page 12

Nancy Robertson, page 27

Joan Robinson, page 110

Spencer Smith, page 37

Captain Brenda Thomas, pages 60, 70, 71, 73, 121

Mario Toti, page 81

Eric Washburn, page 70

Linda Wood, pages 10, 15

Additional photography courtesy of:
Andrew Edgar Photography, pages 35, 65, 87, 103

iStock, pages 46, 53, 75, 85, 115, 143

Maine Windjammer Cruises, pages 50, 51, 54, 110, 112, 116

Windjammer *Angelique*, page 40

Schooner *Lewis R. French*, pages 80, 82, 86

Schooner *Mary Day*, pages 80, 90, 91, 95, 96, 97

Schooner *Stephen Taber*, pages 1, 6, 20, 25, 26, 130, 131

Schooner *Victory Chimes*, pages 140, 141

Index